THE
MYTH
OF A CHRISTIAN
NATION

GREGORY A. BOYD

THE
MYTH
OF A CHRISTIAN
NATION

HOW THE QUEST FOR POLITICAL POWER
IS DESTROYING THE CHURCH

ZONDERVAN®

GRAND RAPIDS, MICHIGAN 49530 USA

ZONDERVAN.COM/
AUTHORTRACKER

ZONDERVAN®

The Myth of a Christian Nation
Copyright © 2005 by Gregory A. Boyd

Requests for information should be addressed to:
Zondervan, *Grand Rapids, Michigan 49530*

Library of Congress Cataloging-in-Publication Data
Boyd, Gregory A.
    The myth of a Christian nation : how the quest for political power is destroying
the church / Gregory A. Boyd.— 1st ed.
      p. cm.
    Includes bibliographical references.
    ISBN-13: 978-0-310-26730-0
    ISBN-10: 0-310-26730-7
    1. Evangelicalism—United States. 2. Christianity and politics—United States.
3. Conservatism—Religious aspects—Christianity. 4. Kingdom of God. I. Title.
BR1642.U5B69 2006
322'.10973—dc22

          2005030108

Interior design by Beth Shagene

Printed in the United States of America

---

06 07 08 09 10 11 12 • 21 20 19 18 17 16 15 14 13 12 11 10 9 8 7 6

To my wonderful stepmother,
Jeanne Boyd.
Your love, patience, and understanding
made the last two decades
of my father's life his best.
What a gift you are!
All of us kids love and appreciate you
more than words can say.

CONTENTS

HOW THIS BOOK CAME TO BE— AND WHY IT MAY IRRITATE SOME READERS

LIKE MANY EVANGELICAL PASTORS IN THE MONTHS BEFORE THE 2004 election, I felt pressure from a number of right-wing political and religious sources, as well as from some people in my own congregation, to "shepherd my flock" into voting for "the right candidate" and "the right position." Among other things, I was asked to hand out leaflets, to draw attention to various political events, and to have our church members sign petitions, make pledges, and so on. Increasingly, some in our church grew irate because of my refusal (supported by the church board) to have the church participate in these activities.

In April of 2004, as the religious buzz was escalating, I felt it necessary to preach a series of sermons that would provide a biblical explanation for why our church should not join the rising chorus of right-wing political activity. I also decided this would be a good opportunity to expose the danger of associating the Christian faith too closely with any political point of view, whether conservative or liberal. I had touched on this topic several times in the past but never as deeply, clearly, and persistently. The series was entitled "The Cross and the Sword," and it forms the foundation for this book.

The response surprised me. For one thing, I had never received so much positive feedback. Some people literally wept with gratitude, saying that they had always felt like outsiders in the evangelical community for not "toeing the conservative party line." Others reported that their eyes had been opened to how they had unwittingly allowed political and national agendas to cloud their vision of the uniquely beautiful kingdom of God.

But neither had I ever received so much intensely negative feedback. I felt as though I'd stuck a stick in a hornet's nest! About 20 percent of my congregation (roughly a thousand people) left the church.[1]

Many who left sincerely believe there is little ambiguity in how true Christian faith translates into politics. Since God is against abortion, Christians should vote for the pro-life candidate, they believe—and the preacher should say so. Since God is against homosexuality, Christians should vote for the candidate who supports the marriage amendment act—and a Bible-believing pastor should proclaim this. Since God is for personal freedom, Christians should vote for the candidate who will fulfill "America's mission" to bring freedom to the world—and any American pastor, like myself, should use his "God-given authority and responsibility" to make this known. "It's *that* simple," I was told. To insist that it's *not*, some suggested, is to be (as I was variously described) a liberal, a compromiser, wishy-washy, unpatriotic, afraid to take a stand, or simply on the side of Satan.

Some readers undoubtedly share these convictions and may already be responding negatively to this book. Like many American evangelicals, you may assume that espousing a certain political position is simply *part of what it means* to be Christian. It may be difficult for you to fathom how an evangelical pastor could, for theological reasons, refuse to use the pulpit to support a pro-life, pro-family, pro-Christian values, pro-American political platform. Aren't we supposed to be trying to take America back for God? Consequently, you too may be tempted to write me off as liberal, a compromiser, wishy-washy, unpatriotic, afraid to take a stand, or on the side of Satan. If so, let me assure you that, for all my shortcomings, I don't believe any of those labels accurately describes me.

And I'd ask you to hear me out.

At the outset, I want you to know I appreciate and respect your convictions. I understand the consternation you may feel, but at the same time, I challenge you to keep an open mind and to consider this book's arguments. I know how difficult it is to take a book seriously when it confronts one's most cherished beliefs. I also know that few things in life are as intellectually and spiritually beneficial as forcing ourselves to consider ideas different from our own—even ideas that may irritate and offend.

This book may well irritate and offend you at times. You may never agree with me. But I believe that wrestling with these issues will benefit you nonetheless. I only ask that you hear me out.

THE CENTRAL THESIS OF THIS BOOK

My thesis, which caused such an uproar, is this: I believe a significant segment of American evangelicalism is guilty of nationalistic and political idolatry. To a frightful degree, I think, evangelicals fuse the kingdom of God with a preferred version of the kingdom of the world (whether it's our national interests, a particular form of government, a particular political program, or so on). Rather than focusing our understanding of God's kingdom on the person of Jesus—who, incidentally, never allowed himself to get pulled into the political disputes of his day—I believe many of us American evangelicals have allowed our understanding of the kingdom of God to be polluted with political ideals, agendas, and issues.

For some evangelicals, the kingdom of God is largely about, if not centered on, "taking America back for God," voting for the Christian candidate, outlawing abortion, outlawing gay marriage, winning the culture war, defending political freedom at home and abroad, keeping the phrase "under God" in the Pledge of Allegiance, fighting for prayer in the public schools and at public events, and fighting to display the Ten Commandments in government buildings.

I will argue that this perspective is misguided, that fusing together the kingdom of God with this or any other version of the kingdom of the world is idolatrous and that this fusion is having serious negative consequences for Christ's church and for the advancement of God's kingdom.

I do *not* argue that those political positions are either wrong or right. Nor do I argue that Christians shouldn't be involved in politics. While people whose faith has been politicized may well interpret me along such lines, I assure you that this is not what I'm saying. The issue is far more fundamental than how we should vote or participate in government. Rather, I hope to challenge the assumption that finding the right political path has anything to do with advancing the kingdom of God.

THE FOUNDATIONAL MYTH

What gives the connection between Christianity and politics such strong emotional force in the U.S.? I believe it is the longstanding myth that America is a Christian nation.[2]

From the start, we have tended to believe that God's will was manifested in the conquest and founding of our country—and that it is still manifested in our actions around the globe. Throughout our history, most Americans have assumed our nation's causes and wars were righteous and just, and that "God is on our side." In our minds—as so often in our sanctuaries—the cross and the American flag stand side by side. Our allegiance to God tends to go hand in hand with our allegiance to country. Consequently, many Christians who take their faith seriously see themselves as the religious guardians of a Christian homeland. America, they believe, is a holy city "set on a hill," and the church's job is to keep it shining.[3]

The negative reaction to my sermons made it clear that this foundational myth is alive and well in the evangelical community—and not just in its fundamentalist fringes. That reaction leads me to suspect that this myth is being embraced more intensely and widely now than in the past precisely because evangelicals sense that it is being threatened.[4] The truth is that the concept of America as a Christian nation, with all that accompanies that myth, is actually losing its grip on the collective national psyche, and as America becomes increasingly pluralistic and secularized, the civil religion of Christianity is losing its force. Understandably, this produces consternation among those who identify themselves as the nation's religious guardians.

So, when the shepherd of a flock of these religious guardians stands up—in the pulpit no less—and suggests that this foundational American myth is, in fact, untrue, that America is not now and never was a Christian nation, that God is not necessarily on America's side, and that the kingdom of God we are called to advance is not about "taking America back for God"—well, for some, that's tantamount to going AWOL.

I respect the sincerity of that conviction, but for me, it simply confirms how badly the church needs to hear the message of this book.

The myth of America as a Christian nation, with the church as its guardian, has been, and continues to be, damaging both to the church and to the advancement of God's kingdom. Among other things, this nationalistic myth blinds us to the way in which our most basic and most cherished cultural assumptions are diametrically opposed to the kingdom way of life taught by Jesus and his disciples. Instead of living out the radically countercultural mandate of the kingdom of God, this myth has inclined us to Christianize many pagan aspects of our culture. Instead of providing the culture with a radically alternative way of life, we largely present it with a religious version of what it already is. The myth clouds our vision of God's distinctly beautiful kingdom and thereby undermines our motivation to live as set-apart (holy) disciples of this kingdom.

Even more fundamentally, because this myth links the kingdom of God with certain political stances within American politics, it has greatly compromised the holy beauty of the kingdom of God to non-Christians. This myth harms the church's primary mission. For many in America and around the world, the American flag has smothered the glory of the cross, and the ugliness of our American version of Caesar has squelched the radiant love of Christ. Because the myth that America is a Christian nation has led many to associate America with Christ, many now hear the good news of Jesus only as American news, capitalistic news, imperialistic news, exploitive news, antigay news, or Republican news. And whether justified or not, many people want nothing to do with any of it.

TWO CONTRASTING KINGDOMS

In the pages that follow, I'll suggest that the kingdom Jesus came to establish is "not from this world" (John 18:36), for it operates differently than the governments of the world do. While all the versions of the kingdom of the world acquire and exercise power *over* others, the kingdom of God, incarnated and modeled in the person of Jesus Christ, advances only by exercising power *under* others.[5] It expands by manifesting the power of self-sacrificial, Calvary-like love.

To put it differently, the governments of the world seek to establish, protect, and advance their ideals and agendas. It's in the fallen nature of all those governments to want to "win." By contrast, the kingdom Jesus established and modeled with his life, death, and resurrection doesn't seek to "win" by any criteria the world would use. Rather, it seeks to be faithful. It demonstrates the reign of God by manifesting the sacrificial character of God, and in the process, it reveals the most beautiful, dynamic, and transformative power in the universe. It testifies that this power alone—the power to transform people from the inside out by coming *under* them—holds the hope of the world. Everything the church is about, I argue, hangs on preserving the radical uniqueness of this kingdom in contrast to the kingdom of the world.

THREE PRELIMINARY WORDS

But three preliminary words need to be said.

First, my thesis applies as much to Christians on the political left as on the political right.[6] While I'm concerned about the fusion of the two kingdoms from both sides, the focus of this book is more on the political right, since that political orientation is far and away the dominant one among evangelicals at this point in history. The political right currently has far more religious and political clout—and has captured far more of the media spotlight. For that reason, it warrants more attention.

Second, to insist that we keep the kingdom of God radically distinct from all versions of the kingdom of the world does not mean that our faith and moral convictions shouldn't inform our participation in the political process. Of course they should—but that is true of all citizens in a free country. Whether we're aware of it or not, all of us, whether religious or not, vote our faith and values.[7]

What the distinction between the two kingdoms does imply, however, is that citizens of the kingdom of God need to take care to distinguish between their core faith and values on the one hand and the *particular way* they politically express their faith and values on the other. While the way of the kingdom of God is always simple, straightforward, and uncompromising, the way of the kingdom of the world is always complex, ambiguous, and inevitably full of compromises. Hence, kingdom people who share the same core faith and values can and often do disagree about how their faith and values should inform their involvement in the kingdom of the world.

Finally, this book is written to help us get a clear vision of the unique kingdom of God as revealed in the life of Jesus, to see how its Calvary-like way of bringing about change in people's lives and in society is completely different from the world's, and to see the great harm that results when Jesus' disciples fail to preserve the uniqueness of that way. This book does not attempt to resolve all ambiguities between these two kingdoms

The purpose of this book, rather, is to cast a broad vision of the kingdom of God and show its stark contrast to the kingdom of the world. If it helps some readers see how wonderfully different God's kingdom is from the world; if it helps some place more trust in God's unique "power under" mode of operation; and if it motivates some to become more committed to living out the radically alternative, countercultural life of this kingdom—it will have served its purpose.

CHAPTER 1

THE KINGDOM OF THE SWORD

My kingdom is not from this world.

JOHN 18:36

The kings of the Gentiles lord it over them; and those in authority
over them are called benefactors. But not so with you.

LUKE 22:25–26

For the church to be a community that does not need war in order to give
itself purpose and virtue puts the church at odds with nations.... The battle is one
we fight with the gospel weapons of witness and love, not violence and coercion.

HAUERWAS AND WILLIMON[1]

SHORTLY AFTER JESUS' ARREST, PILATE ASKED HIM, "ARE YOU THE KING
of the Jews?" (John 18:33). To be a king, one must have a kingdom
—a king's domain—and Pilate wanted to know if Jesus thought the
Jews were his domain. It was a straightforward question, requiring
a simple yes or no.

But Jesus, typically, did not give the expected response. Rather,
he told Pilate that his kingdom "is not from this world" (John
18:36).

Pilate assumed Jesus' kingdom could be understood on the same
terms as every other earthly kingdom—along geographical, ethnic, nationalistic, and ideological lines. But he was mistaken. Jesus'
kingdom is radically unlike any kingdom, government, or political
ideology in the world. To appreciate Jesus' radically unique kingdom, we need to know about the worldly kingdoms it stands in
contrast to.

THE "POWER OVER" KINGDOM

Wherever a person or group exercises power over others—or tries to—*there* is a version of the kingdom of the world. While it comes in many forms, the kingdom of the world is in essence a "power over" kingdom. In some versions—such as America—subjects have a say in who their rulers will be, while in others they have none. In some versions, subjects may influence how their rulers exercise power over them—for example, what laws they will live by—while in others they do not. There have been democratic, socialist, communist, fascist, and totalitarian versions of the kingdom of the world, but they all share this distinctive characteristic: they exercise "power over" people.

I refer to the power that the kingdom of the world wields as "the power of the sword." I'm not referring to a literal sword necessarily—though that has often been true—but rather, to the ability of those in power to inflict pain on those who threaten or defy their authority. The power of the sword is the ability to coerce behavior by threats and to make good on those threats when necessary: if a law is broken, you will be punished. Of course, the laws of the different versions of the kingdom of the world vary greatly, but the raised sword behind the laws gives them their power, and that keeps every version of the kingdom of the world intact.

Though all versions of the kingdom of the world try to influence how their subjects think and feel, their power resides in their ability to control behavior. As effective as a raised sword is in producing conformity, it cannot bring about an internal change. A kingdom can stipulate that murder will be punished, for example, but it can't change a person's desire to murder. It may be that the only reason a person refrains from killing is because he or she doesn't want to be imprisoned or executed. Their motives may be entirely self-serving. The kingdom of the world doesn't really care, so long as the person conforms to the law. Laws, enforced by the sword, control behavior but cannot change hearts.

GOD AND THE KINGDOM OF THE WORLD

The "power over" that all versions of the kingdom of the world exercise is not altogether bad. Were the world not fallen, the threat of the sword would be unnecessary. The sword is part of our common curse, yet God uses it to keep law and order in the world. For this reason, followers of Jesus are to be obedient, as far as possible, to whatever government they find in power over them. The apostle Paul puts it this way:

> Let every person be subject to the governing authorities; for there is no authority except from God, and those authorities that exist have been instituted [*tetagmenai*] by God.... Rulers are not a terror to good conduct, but to bad. Do you wish to have no fear of the authority? Then do what is good, and you will receive its approval; for it is God's servant for your good. But if you do what is wrong, you should be afraid, for the authority does not bear the sword in vain! It is the servant of God to execute wrath on the wrongdoer. (Rom. 13:1, 3–4)

The government "does not bear the sword in vain," therefore, for it is a divine means of keeping fallen people from wreaking havoc on each other. God's intent is to use any given "power over" government as his "servant for ... good." This doesn't mean that worldly governments are created by God or that governments always use their God-given authority as God intended—as though Hitler and Stalin were carrying out God's will! Paul rather says that God institutes, directs, or stations (*tetagmenai*) governments. John Howard Yoder's comment is insightful:

> God is not said to *create* or ... *ordain* the powers that be, but only to *order* them, to put them in order, sovereignly to tell them where they belong, what is their place. It is not as if there was a time when there was no government and then God made government through a new creative intervention;

there has been hierarchy and authority and power since human society existed. Its exercise has involved domination, disrespect for human dignity, and real or potential violence ever since sin has existed. Nor is it that by ordering this realm God specifically, morally approves of what a government does. The sergeant does not produce the soldiers he drills; the librarian does not create nor approve of the book she or he catalogs and shelves. Likewise God does not take the responsibility for the existence of the rebellious "powers that be" or for their shape or identity; they already are. What the text says is that God orders them, brings them into line, providentially and permissively lines them up with divine purpose.[2]

As he did with nations in the Old Testament (for instance, in Isaiah 10), God uses governments as he finds them, in all their ungodly rebellious ways, to serve his own providential purposes. As Paul describes in Romans 13, this general purpose is to preserve as much law and order as is possible. Insofar as governments do this, they are properly exercising the authority God grants them and are, to that extent, good.

Because of this good function, disciples of Jesus are commanded to "honor the emperor" (1 Peter 2:17) and live in conformity to the laws of their land as much as possible—that is, insofar as those laws do not conflict with our calling as citizens of the kingdom of God (Rom. 13:1; Titus 3:1; 1 Peter 2:13–17; and specifically Acts 5:29). Whether we find ourselves in a democratic, socialist, or communist country, we are to pray for our leaders and seek to live in peace in that country (1 Tim. 2:1–3). We are, in a word, to be good citizens of whatever version of the kingdom of the world we find ourselves in.

SATAN AND THE KINGDOM OF THE WORLD

But we need to know another important dimension of the biblical teaching about the kingdom of the world. While God directs governments for the good of fallen people, Scripture also teaches that another cosmic force exists, one that is hostile to God and influences governments to accomplish evil. Indeed, sometimes the scope of authority granted to this cosmic adversary, Satan, in Scripture is astounding.

For example, in Luke 4 the Devil tempted Jesus by showing him "all the kingdoms of the world" while saying, "To you I will give their glory and all this authority; for *it has been given over to me*, and *I give it to anyone I please*. If you, then, will worship me, it will all be yours" (Luke 4:5–7, emphasis added). Jesus, of course, would not worship the Devil to acquire these kingdoms. But note: he doesn't dispute the Devil's claim to own them.

Apparently, the authority of all the kingdoms of the world has been given to Satan. It's not clear from this text whether we humans gave the Devil this authority when we surrendered to him in the Garden (Genesis 3) or whether God originally entrusted Lucifer with this authority before he rebelled. What is clear is that, however it came about, God's cosmic archenemy now owns the authority of all versions of the kingdom of the world and gives this authority to whomever he pleases.

This teaching is in various ways found throughout the New Testament. John goes so far as to claim that "the whole world lies under the power of the evil one" (1 John 5:19) and refers to all the kingdoms of the world as a single kingdom under demonic rule that is in the process of being delivered over to Jesus (Rev. 11:15). This kingdom is symbolized as "Babylon," the violent world empire that opposes God at every turn, in the book of Revelation.[3] Her servants are the world's rulers, and "all nations" are "deceived" by her "sorcery" (Rev. 18:23)—the deceptive lure of power. Certainly some governments are better than others, for they carry out God's purpose of preserving law and order better than others. But no earthly kingdom, however good, is exempt from the scriptural teaching that it is part of "Babylon," a worldwide kingdom ruled by Satan.

Along these same lines, Jesus three times refers to Satan as the "ruler of this world" (John 12:31; 14:30; 16:11). The term "ruler" (*arche*) was a political term used to denote the highest ruling authority in a given region—and Jesus applied it to Satan over the whole world! Functionally, Satan is the acting CEO of all earthly governments. Paul agrees, for he refers to Satan as "the god of this age" and as "the ruler of the power of the air" (2 Cor. 4:4; Eph. 2:2). We see, then, that while God ultimately gives authority to governments to preserve law and order in a fallen world, and while God orders and orchestrates governments as he finds them to his own providential advantage, Satan—"the destroyer" who "deceives the nations" (Rev. 9:11; 20:3, 8; especially 13:14)—is heavily involved in all of them and works at cross-purposes to God.

I know of no way to resolve the ambiguity involved in this dual analysis of the kingdom of the world—but simply recognizing that there is, at the very least, a strong demonic presence polluting all versions of the kingdom of the world has to significantly affect how followers of Jesus view earthly governments. Minimally, this recognition implies that we can never assume that any particular nation—including our own—is always, or even usually, aligned with God. We may be thankful whenever our government wields the sword in ways that are just and that punish wrongdoers. But we must also always remember that fallen principalities and powers (Eph. 2:2; 6:12) strongly influence our government, and every government, however relatively good that government may otherwise be.

To accept this teaching means that, while believers should strive to be good citizens, praying and working for peace and justice, they must always practice a healthy suspicion toward the "power over," sword-wielding government they are subject to. While a particular political ideology may be better than others at preserving justice, law, and order, we must never forget that even the best political ideology lies under the influence of a "power over" cosmic ruler who is working at cross-purposes to God.

THE GODS AND FALLEN PASSION

When we accept that the destroyer who has been "a murderer from the beginning" (John 8:44) is the functional ruler of all versions of the kingdom of the world, we can make sense of the fact that the history of the world has been one of violent conflict. In all of recorded history, only a few decades have seen no major wars—and even during these times of relative peace, much local violence existed. Historians estimate that in the twentieth century alone over 200 million people died as a result of war and political conflict. The history of the world is a massive river of blood, and this waste of life testifies not only to the violent tendencies of the fallen human heart but to the destructive nature of the ruler of the kingdom of this world.

Homer's *Iliad* and *Odyssey* brilliantly capture the violent nature of Babylon. In Homer, as in much Greek tragedy, humans are driven by passions they can't completely control—passions to secure and acquire power and possessions, to sacrifice for (and to) certain gods, to uphold religious traditions, to acquire a personal legacy, to protect loved ones, and to advance the cause of tribe or nation. The trouble is that other people have their own power they want to secure and expand, their own possessions they want to acquire and protect, their own gods to sacrifice to, their own traditions to defend, their own legacies to build, and, perhaps most importantly, their own tribal and national interests to advance. This, for Homer, means that sooner or later, war is inevitable.

Furthermore, in Homer "the gods" are always involved in the affairs of humans. Some gods, for their own reasons, inflame certain individuals with passions that lead them one way, while other gods, for their own reasons, inflame other individuals with passions that lead them an opposite way—and the result is a bloodbath. For Homer, the inevitability of war is not just the result of conflicting passions—it has a supernatural dimension.

And all the while, Zeus sits on Mount Olympus, amused by the sport of it all.

The brilliance of Homer's *Iliad* and *Odyssey* lies in how powerfully they express truth, especially when understood from a scriptural perspective. We fallen humans have passionate convictions that control us and lead us into conflict with others who have equally passionate convictions. We believe in *our* nation over and against *their* nation, *our* religion over and against *their* religion, *our* culture over and against *their* culture, *our* political ideology over and against *their* political ideology, and so on. And insofar as we are influenced by the kingdom of the world, we express these passions by attempting to exercise "power over" others as their nation, culture, religion, or political ideology conflicts with or threatens our own. Violence is the inevitable result.

Homer was also right about the gods. Though secular people give it no credence, from a scriptural perspective we have to grant that our tribal, territorial, and ideological passions have a demonic dimension to them. The Bible speaks much of rebellious gods, fallen principalities, powers, and demons that affect what comes to pass in this world. There are gods over particular nations that are not on God's side and thus do not exercise their dominion in ways that promote peace and justice. From a scriptural perspective, these fallen gods are behind and involved in the conflict that occurs between nations.[4]

And all the while, Satan, the ultimate "power over" god of this age, watches the bloodshed with a demonic sense of amusement.

THE TIT-FOR-TAT KINGDOM

It's hard not to get pulled into the fallen passions that fuel the violence of the kingdom of the world. Indeed, the demonic, tribalistic passion that sets "us" over against "them" seems completely natural to us in our fallen condition. If you hit me, my natural (fallen) instinct is to hit you back—not turn the other cheek! Tit for tat, eye for an eye, tooth for a tooth—this is what makes the bloody kingdom of the world go around.

To illustrate, in 2004 it was revealed that a number of American soldiers inflicted horrendous, humiliating abuse on Iraqi soldiers at Abu Gharib prison. A few days after the pictures and videos of the terrible abuse were made public, Iraqi terrorists made their own macabre film showing the grotesque beheading of an American civilian, John Berg. In the film, they told us that they executed Mr. Berg in response to the brutality endured by their own soldiers at Abu Gharib, and they vowed to continue "because we are a people of vengeance." At the time of this writing, they have been true to their vow.

When Americans learned of the beheading, most were inflamed with a sense of hatred. The internet was flooded with emails and websites calling for vengeance — an eye for an eye, a head for a head. The life of John Berg had to be atoned for and the honor of our nation had to be restored. Recall how *you* felt when you heard or saw what happened to Mr. Berg or others at the hands of the terrorists.

Your yearning for justice is, of course, natural. But this rage is exactly what led the terrorists to cut off Mr. Berg's head in the first place. You probably passionately believe that our cause is just and theirs is evil, but the terrorists passionately believe their cause is just and ours is evil. Your passion for American justice is mirrored by their passion for Islamic justice. If, for a moment, you can suspend the question of whose justice is really right and step inside the national and religious passions of the terrorists, you'll understand the world of Homer — and understand what drives the kingdom of the world. You can begin to understand why, given *our* passionate convictions and given *their* passionate convictions, this bloody tit-for-tat game is almost inevitable. *Our* particular tribal, national, religious, and political passions directly conflict with *their* tribal, national, religious, and political passions, and this gives birth to a shared sense of righteous indignation willing to violently crush each other.

At the same time, it's important to remember that history itself always feeds our conflicting passions. Much of the profound animosity Islamic terrorists feel towards "satanic" America is fueled by a cultural memory of what Christians did to Muslims during the Crusades. Believing that America is a Christian nation, they direct their collective, historically acquired hatred toward it. Now, you might be tempted to respond by saying, "Well, *they* did a lot of bad stuff to Christians throughout history as well" — and you'd be right. But this is exactly the sort of thinking that fuels the endless tit-for-tat kingdom of the world. You naturally believe your tribe

(Christians/America) is at least a bit less guilty than the opposition, and this is exactly what they believe about their tribe. And so the bloody game goes on, as it has in one form or another across the globe and throughout history. Under the rule of Satan and other fallen gods, Babylon has reigned on the earth since the original rebellion.

And all the while, the "power over" god of this age smiles with demonic amusement.

A DIFFERENT KIND OF KINGDOM

Fallen humans tend to identify their own group as righteous and any group that opposes them as evil. If *they* were not evil, we tend to believe, no conflict would exist. Hence, the only way to end the conflict is to "rid the world of this evil," as President George W. Bush said after the terrorist attack on the World Trade Center. The "good" (our tribe) must extinguish the "evil" (their tribe), using all means necessary, including violence. This is the age-old "myth of redemptive violence."[5]

The true cause of violence, of course, is not "the enemy" but something much more fundamental, something both we and our enemy have in common. The true cause lies in the fact that our fallen hearts are idolatrous and subject to the fallen powers that influence us.

So long as people locate their worth, significance, and security in their power, possessions, traditions, reputations, religious behaviors, tribe, and nation rather than in a relationship with their Creator, Babylon's bloody tit-for-tat game is inevitable. Of course, peaceful solutions must still be sought and can, to some degree, be attained with regard to each particular conflict. But as long as humans define their personal and tribal self-interests over and against other people's competing personal and tribal interests, violence is inevitable and will break out again.

History is filled with people who believed that this or that war would root out evil once and for all and bring about lasting peace.

The myth has been especially strong in American history and has again been invoked in the war against terrorism: We, the righteous nation, will root out all evil. But people who align themselves with the kingdom of God must see through the deception of this nationalistic mantra, for those who live by the sword will die by the sword (Matt. 26:52). The demonic sirocco of violence is fed by the illusion of ultimate "righteous" victory. Any peace achieved by violence is a peace forever threatened by violence, thus ensuring that the bloody game will be perpetuated.

Followers of Jesus must realize—and must help others realize—that the hope of the world lies not in any particular version of the kingdom of the world gaining the upper hand in Babylon's endless tit-for-tat game. The hope of the world lies in a kingdom that is not of this world, a kingdom that doesn't participate in tit for tat, a kingdom that operates with a completely different understanding of power. It is the kingdom established by Jesus Christ and a kingdom that is expanded by people committed to following him. It is the kingdom of God.

The unique nature of this kingdom is revealed in a discussion Jesus had with some of his disciples, who were arguing over which of them would be the greatest in the kingdom of heaven. They were, in their own way, exhibiting the "power over" mindset that characterizes the kingdom of the world and competing with one another to be esteemed. Jesus responded:

> The kings of the Gentiles lord it over them; and those in authority over them are called benefactors. But not so with you; rather the greatest among you must become like the youngest, and the leader like one who serves. For who is greater, the one who is at the table or the one who serves? Is it not the one at the table? But I am among you as one who serves. (Luke 22:25–27)

Jesus identified the disciples' argument as a typical kingdom-of-the-world conflict—and thoroughly pagan. This is the way worldly rulers—and the world in general—naturally think. Indeed, it is a matter of common sense by the world's standards. Naturally the older is greater than the younger, the leader worthy of higher esteem than the follower, the one who sits at the table greater than the one who serves. Yet Jesus not only rejects this "common sense" logic—he reverses it! Jesus, the Son of God, the one who is greatest by any standard, came to earth not to be served but to serve others, and the kingdom he came to establish would be marked by this distinctive feature. It would not be a "power over" kingdom; it would be a "power under" kingdom. It would be a kingdom where greatness is defined by serving and sacrificing for others.

This is why Jesus responded to Pilate's question by saying his kingdom was "not from this world." If his kingdom were of this world, he told Pilate, his followers would fight the way the kingdom of the world always fights (John 18:36). They would use the "power over" tactics and wield the sword to advance their personal, religious, and political interests. They would defend Jesus in the name of God, of righteousness, and of the glory of Israel—but this is not the kind of kingdom Jesus came to establish.

One of his misguided disciples even tried to fight like a kingdom-of-the-world participant, cutting off the ear of one of the soldiers who came to arrest Jesus. Jesus rebuked the disciple and demonstrated the nature of his unique heavenly kingdom by healing the soldier's ear (Luke 22:50–51), showing that his kingdom would advance not by destroying the enemy who seeks to destroy you, but by loving, serving, and hopefully transforming the enemy who seeks to destroy you.

It was the same message Jesus was about to send Pilate and the world. Rather than calling on his disciples or the legions of angels that were at his disposal to exercise "power over" in his defense, Jesus let himself be crucified. Why? Because Pilate and the world needed him to. It was an outrageously loving thing to do—and for this reason it violated the common sense of the kingdom of the world.

The kingdom of Jesus was, and is, a radically different kind of kingdom indeed, and it is this kingdom that all who follow Jesus are called to manifest in every area of their lives.

CHAPTER 2

THE KINGDOM
OF THE CROSS

Love your enemies, do good to those who hate you,
bless those who curse you, pray for those who abuse you.

LUKE 6:27–28

THE MUSTARD-SEED KINGDOM

The heart of Jesus' teaching was "the kingdom of God." He spoke about that topic more frequently than any other, and it pervades all his actions as well.[1] Indeed, the Gospels make it clear that Jesus was the embodiment—the incarnation—of the kingdom of God. When Jesus was present, so was that kingdom (see Matt. 12:28; and especially 3:2; 4:17). Though the world as a whole was and remains part of the domain in which Satan is king, in Jesus the domain in which God is king has been introduced into the world. The central goal of Jesus' life was to plant the seed of this new kingdom so that, like a mustard seed, it would gradually expand. Eventually that kingdom would end the rule of Satan and reestablish God, the Creator of the world, as its rightful ruler (Matt. 13:31–32). In other words, Jesus came to destroy the cosmic "power over" lord and establish the kingdom of God upon the earth (Heb. 2:14; 1 John 3:8).[2]

Jesus planted the seed of the kingdom of God with his ministry, death, and resurrection and then gave to the church, the body of all who submit to his lordship, the task of embodying and living out this distinct kingdom. We are to be nothing less than "the body of Christ," which means, among other things, that we are to do exactly what Jesus did (Rom. 12:4–5; 1 Cor. 10:17; 12:12–27; Eph. 4:4; 5:30; Col. 1:18, 24; 2:19). John teaches us that, "Whoever says, 'I abide in him,' ought to walk *just as he walked*" (1 John

2:6, emphasis added; also 1 John 1:7; 1 Cor. 4:6; 11:1; Eph. 5:1–2; Phil. 3:17; Col. 2:6; 1 Thess. 1:6; 2 Thess. 3:7; 1 Peter 2:21). "Let the same mind be in you that was in Christ Jesus" (Phil. 2:5) must be regarded as our central command. Our every thought, word, and deed is to reflect the character of Jesus and thus manifest the reign of God in the world (see Rom. 12:2; 2 Cor. 10:3–5).

Not only this, but according to the Bible, the community of those who submit to Christ's lordship are in a real sense to *be* Jesus to the world, for through the church Christ himself continues to expand the reign of God in the world.[3] We collectively are his "second" body, as it were, through which he continues to do what he did in his "first" body. Through us, Jesus continues to embody the kingdom of God in the world. Christ dwells in us and among us individually and corporately, and he longs to live *through* us individually and corporately.

By God's design, this is how the kingdom of God expands and transforms the world. As we allow Christ's character to be formed in us—as we think and act like Jesus—others come under the loving influence of the kingdom and eventually their own hearts are won over to the King of Kings. The reign of God is thus established in their hearts, and the kingdom of God expands. That process, Scripture tells us, will culminate in the return of the King accompanied by legions of angels, at which time Satan's rule will end, the earth will be purged of all that is inconsistent with God's rule, and his kingdom of love will be established once and for all.[4]

This, in a nutshell, is the primary thing God is up to in our world. He's not primarily about getting people to pray a magical "sinner's prayer" or to confess certain magical truths as a means of escaping hell. He's not about gathering together a group who happen to believe all the right things. Rather, he's about gathering together a group of people who embody the kingdom—who individually and corporately manifest the reality of the reign of God on the earth. And he's about growing this new kingdom through his body to take over the world. This vision of what God is about lies at the heart of Jesus' ministry, and it couldn't contrast with the kingdom of the world more sharply.

WHAT POWER DO YOU TRUST?

In the words of Barbara Rossing and John Yoder, borrowing an image from the book of Revelation, the contrast between the "power over" kingdom of the world and the "power under" kingdom of God is "Lion power" versus "Lamb power."[5] The kingdom of God advances by people lovingly placing themselves *under* others, in service to others, at cost to themselves. This "coming under" doesn't mean that followers of Jesus conform to other people's wishes, but it does mean that we always interact with others with their best interests in mind.

Following the example of Christ, and in stark contrast to the modus operandi of the world, we are to do "nothing from selfish ambition or conceit, but in humility regard others as better than [our]selves." We are to "look not to [our] own interests, but to the interests of others" (Phil. 2:3–4). We are to "not seek [our] own advantage, but that of the other" (1 Cor. 10:24, cf. 10:33). Following Jesus' example, we are to find honor in washing people's feet (John 13:14–15)—that is, in serving them in any way we can.

So too, in following our Master we are to seek to do good and free all who are "oppressed by the devil" (Acts 10:38) while we voluntarily bear others' burdens (Gal. 6:2). We are to "outdo one another in showing honor" (Rom. 12:10) and never be competitive with others (unless, of course, it's for fun) (Gal. 5:26). We are to "put up with the failings of the weak, and not please ourselves," always asking how we might "please our neighbor for the good purpose of building up the neighbor" (Rom. 15:1–2). We are to feed the hungry, clothe the naked, take in the homeless, befriend the friendless, and visit the condemned prisoner (James 2:15–17; 1 John 3:14–18; cf. Matt. 25:34–40).

All of this involves exercising "power under." We are to engage in this behavior not out of duty to an abstract ethic, but because the life of the one who came under all humanity on Calvary is pumping kingdom life through our veins. We are part of the growing revolutionary kingdom he began and is continuing to grow. It is a kingdom that looks like him, a kingdom in which the greatest is the one who serves others (Matt. 20:26; Luke 22:26–27). It is a kingdom in which the exalted will be humbled, but the humble exalted (Luke 14:11; 18:14). It is a kingdom in which one is blessed when divested of power—is "poor in spirit," "mourns," is "meek," and "persecuted" (Matt. 5:3–5, 10–11)—and even is in the position of socially rejected sinners (Matt. 21:31), for these are the ones who are most open to entering the kind of "power under" life the kingdom has to offer.

While we might regard this kind of power as weak by kingdom-of-the-world criteria, in truth there is no greater power on the planet than self-sacrificial love. Coming under others has a power to do what laws and bullets and bombs can never do—namely, bring about transformation in an enemy's heart. This is the unique "Lamb power" of the kingdom of God, and indeed, this is the power of God Almighty. When God flexes his omnipotent muscle, it doesn't look like Rambo or the Terminator—it looks like Calvary! And living in this Calvary-like love moment by moment, in all circumstances and in relation to all people, is the sole calling of those who are aligned with the kingdom that Jesus came to bring.

Participants in the kingdom of the world trust the power of the sword to control behavior; participants of the kingdom of God trust the power of self-sacrificial love to transform hearts. The kingdom of the world is concerned with preserving law and order by force; the kingdom of God is concerned with establishing the rule of God through love. The kingdom of the world is centrally concerned with what people *do*; the kingdom of God is centrally concerned with how people *are* and what they can *become.* The kingdom of the world is characterized by judgment; the kingdom of God is characterized by outrageous, even scandalous, grace.

Obviously, when hearts and motives are transformed, behavior is eventually transformed as well—but without "power over" threats. Similarly, where the rule of God is established, law and order are established—but without "power over" force. The kingdom of God accomplishes what the kingdom of the world seeks to accomplish, but it also accomplishes much more, for it transforms people from the inside out—from their heart to their behavior. It has no concern with controlling behavior as an end in itself, such as the kingdom of the world has.

The crucial distinction between the two kingdoms is how they provide antithetical answers to the questions of what power one should trust to change ourselves and others: Do you trust "power over" or "power under"? Do you trust the power of the sword, the power of external force, or do you trust the influential but noncoercive power of Calvary-like love? Do you trust threats, judgment, shame, or social pressure (even in church!) to change people, or do you trust the Holy Spirit working in the people's hearts and using Christlike acts of love to bring about change? The kingdom of God consists of all those who choose the latter rather than the former and who act accordingly. It is composed of people who place God's will above their own and who believe that he will use their sacrificial love for others to expand his kingdom in their lives and in the world.

THE KINGDOM OF THE CROSS

The love we are called to trust and emulate is supremely manifested in the cross of Jesus. The cross is the ultimate symbol of the kingdom of God, for it defines what that kingdom always looks like. It looks like Christ—self-sacrificial and loving. It looks like grace.

As we noted in the previous chapter, Jesus could have exercised "power over" Pilate and the Roman government to defend himself. He could have allowed his disciples to pick up swords and fight, and he could have summoned legions of warrior angels. He could have "won"! Had he done so, he would have preserved his life and controlled the behavior of his foes, but he would not have transformed anyone's heart. He would not have helped anyone love God or love themselves and others as people loved by God. The power of the sword, even if wielded by mighty warring angels, can never transform a person's inner being. While the use of the sword tends to deepen the resolve of the punished rather than transform it,

Jesus' aim was to transform hearts and, by that means, transform the world.

So rather than fight and "win," Jesus chose to "lose." Or better, he chose to lose by kingdom-of-the-world standards so that he might win by kingdom-of-God standards. His trust was not in the power of the sword but in the power of radical, self-sacrificial love, and so he let himself be crucified. Three days later, God vindicated his trust in the power of sacrificial love. He had carried out God's will and, by his sacrifice, defeated death and the forces of evil that hold this world in bondage (Col. 2:13–15).[6]

This is the heart of the kingdom of God. The rule of God is established wherever God's will is obeyed and God's character is manifested. These are, in fact, two facets of the same reality, for God's will is that his character, his "name," or his glory be manifested (see John 12:28; 13:32; 17:1), which is all about displaying God's unsurpassable love (1 John 4:8–9, 16; cf. 3:16). Throughout eternity, God has existed as the perfect love of the Father, Son, and Holy Spirit. When this love is turned outward toward humanity, it looks like Calvary, which perfectly expresses the loving nature and rule of God in a way that legions of angels or a band of fighting disciples would not.

The character and rule of God is manifested when instead of employing violence against his enemies to crush them, Jesus loves his enemies in order to redeem them. The kingdom is revealed when instead of protecting himself, Jesus allows himself to be murdered. God's love is marvelously put on display when instead of clinging to his perfect holiness, Jesus puts himself in the place of sinners. And the nature and rule of God shines radiantly in Jesus' final prayer for the forgiveness of those who moments earlier mocked him, spit on him, whipped him, and crucified him (Luke 23:34).

In all of this, Jesus revealed God's character and God's reign, for all of it disclosed that God loves humanity with the love eternally expressed in the Trinity. In love, God wants to serve humanity by reconciling us to himself, whatever the cost. God places himself under us, despite our sin, to save us and transform us into the image of Jesus. Nothing could be further from the "power over" mindset that characterizes the kingdom of the world.

THE KINGDOM THAT IS JESUS

While the cross most profoundly epitomizes what is true about Jesus, the heart of the kingdom of God is also displayed throughout Jesus' entire life and ministry, which all had a Calvary quality to it.[7] Jesus embodied the kingdom of God; his very identity was about serving others—at cost to himself.

Indeed, the fact that Jesus was willing to become human in the first place manifests the self-sacrificial nature of God's rule. Though he was by nature God, Paul tells us, Jesus didn't cling to this divine status but rather emptied himself, entered into solidarity with fallen humanity, and became a humble servant (Phil. 2:5–8). Though he was rich, Paul says elsewhere, for our sake he became poor (2 Cor. 8:9). He could have remained in the bliss of his perfect loving relationship with the Father and the Spirit, but instead he willingly became a baby born as a social outcast to an unwed mother in a dirty, smelly stable crowded with animals. As Yoder notes, Jesus could have chosen "the untrammeled exercise of sovereign power in the affairs of that humanity amid which he came to dwell," but instead he renounced this and chose to humble himself by becoming a servant of the world.[8] *This* is what the kingdom of God looks like.

Jesus' life and ministry consistently reveal the humble character of a servant. Though he rightfully owned the entire cosmos, he, by choice, had no place to lay his head (Matt. 8:20). Though he rightfully should have been honored by the world's most esteemed dignitaries, he chose to fellowship with tax collectors, drunkards, prostitutes, and other socially unacceptable sinners (Matt. 11:19; Mark 2:15; Luke 5:29–30; 15:1; cf. Luke 7:31–50). Though he rightfully could have demanded service and worship from all, he served the lame and the sick by healing them, the demonized by delivering them, and the outcasts by befriending them. *This* is what the kingdom of God looks like. It looks like humility. It looks like grace. It looks like service. It looks like Jesus.

BECOME AS CHILDREN

Several episodes in Jesus' ministry illustrate this unique nature of the kingdom of God in particularly poignant ways. At one point people brought their children to be blessed by Jesus, but his disciples put a quick stop to it. In typical kingdom-of-the-world fashion, the disciples assumed Jesus was too important to concern himself with children. Jesus showed how wrong-headed they were—and by allowing the children to come to him, he demonstrated the kind of kingdom he came to bring. (I imagine Jesus roaring with laughter as the kids climbed all over him!) To Jesus' way of thinking, there is no place in the kingdom for evaluating how important someone is on the basis of their power, possessions, money, or social respect. Children have none of these, but for that reason, they have open access to the Creator of the universe in his incarnate form.

Elsewhere Jesus announced that the kingdom of God belonged to "such as these" (Matt. 19:14). Unless adults become "like children," Jesus taught, they cannot enter the kingdom of heaven (Matt. 18:3–4). On one occasion he gave a version of this teaching in response to a dispute some disciples were having over who was the "greatest"—typical kingdom-of-the-world antics (Luke 9:46). In the kingdom of God, the least are the greatest and the greatest are the least. Children illustrate this perfectly. Because they are regarded as the least important (especially in first-century Jewish culture), they are, in fact, the greatest—precisely because they are least by kingdom-of-the-world standards. (Jesus' preference for those who were poor, outsiders, downtrodden, and despised teaches the same truth.)

More specifically, children illustrate the nature of the kingdom of God because they have not yet been conditioned to believe they need power, money, and social respect to be great. Nor have they yet learned the worldly principle that one has to trust in and employ "power over" others to acquire and secure these things. In short, they have not yet been socialized into the kingdom-of-the-world mindset. Their minds haven't yet been conformed to "the pattern of this world" (Rom. 12:2 NIV); they are yet humble and innocent. For adults to participate in the kingdom of God, Jesus is saying, we must become deconditioned from kingdom-of-the-world thinking and acting, and return to the humility and innocence of little children.

GOD WASHES FEET

The kingdom-of-God lifestyle was also beautifully illustrated just before the Last Supper. John tells us that Jesus knew that "the Father had given all things into his hands, and that he had come from God and was going to God" (John 13:3). So what did Jesus do with all this divine authority? He "got up from the table, took off his outer robe, and tied a towel around himself. Then he poured water into a basin and began to wash the disciples' feet and to wipe them with the towel that was tied around him" (John 13:4–5).

Here is Jesus, possessing all power in heaven and earth and knowing he is about to be betrayed and die a horrible death—and what does he do? He assumes the position of a common household servant and washes his disciples' dirty, smelly feet—the very people he knows will betray and forsake him before morning!

This is how power is wielded in the kingdom of God. If you have all power in heaven and earth, use it to wash the feet of someone you know will betray you! In serving like this, Jesus declares to all who are willing to hear that he "would not rule by a sword, but by a towel."[9]

HEALING THE EAR OF AN ENEMY

As I've mentioned, the same power of Calvary was manifested several hours later in the Garden of Gethsemane. As temple guards were about to arrest Jesus, Peter drew his sword and cut off the ear of Malchus, the slave of the high priest (John 18:10). This is predictable tit-for-tat behavior in the kingdom of the world: when you're threatened, defend yourself with force. It's significant to note that Peter was always the one who most resisted Jesus' servanthood model of the Messiah. Like many others, Peter held the notion that the Messiah would be a political and military leader who would exercise "power over" the Romans and free Israel. At one point Jesus even has to rebuke Peter, actually calling him "Satan" because of his obstinate resistance to Jesus' call to suffer (Matt. 16:21–23).

Apparently Peter hadn't yet learned his lesson, for he was still trying to protect Jesus (and his own ideal of a militant Messiah). This time, though, Jesus told him to put his sword away, reminding him that "all who take the sword will perish by the sword" (Matt. 26:52). In the tit-for-tat kingdom of Babylon, violence begets more violence, and Jesus hadn't come to propagate more of *that*. Rather, he came to plant the seed of a kingdom that alone holds the hope of ending all violence.

So, far from using his divine authority to fight back, calling legions of angels and forcefully controlling his enemy's behavior, Jesus used his divine authority to heal the ear of a man who came to arrest him. Though he could have exercised "power over" the servant, he displayed outrageous, unconditional love instead by coming under him, by serving him. Jesus was saying, in effect, "Though you seek to do me harm, I care about you and will not use my authority to defeat you. Rather I will serve you and heal you."

This kind of power transforms people. We can't be sure, of course, but it's hard to imagine the healed servant not being profoundly affected by this unexpected act of love. Do you think the servant, with whatever ill will he may have harbored toward Jesus on the way to arresting him, continued to harbor it after his encounter with kingdom love? Can you imagine him being among those who spit on Jesus and mocked him? Is it not more likely that he became at least a little more open to God's love and perhaps a little more loving toward others as a result of Jesus' gift? The point is that love, through service, has a power to affect people in ways that "power over" tactics do not, and it is this unique power of self-sacrificial love that most centrally defines the kingdom of God.

Insofar as we trust *this* kind of power and think and act accordingly, we are bearers of the kingdom of God. Insofar as we do not, we are simply participants in the kingdom of the world.

JESUS' TEACHINGS ON KINGDOM LOVE

Jesus taught what he lived and lived what he taught, so we shouldn't be surprised to find Calvary-type love pervading his teaching.

When asked to name the most important commandment, he answered that "all the law and the prophets" hang on loving God with all our heart, soul, and mind, and on loving our neighbor as ourselves (Matt. 22:36–40). By *neighbor* Jesus meant anyone we happen to come upon in need of our service (Luke 10:27–37)—and he says that *everything* hangs on sacrificially loving this person. We can try to obey all the particulars of the law and prophets, such as the Pharisees did, but if love doesn't motivate this aspiration, we haven't even begun to obey the law and the prophets, even if we meticulously follow every command. Love, not religiosity, is the defining mark of the kingdom of God.

This kingdom love that Jesus speaks of always has a Calvary quality to it. While people in the kingdom of the world find it easy to love those who they think deserve it—that's part of the tit-for-tat nature of the world's kingdom—kingdom-of-God participants are called to love all people unconditionally, even their enemies, just as Christ did (Luke 6:27, 35). We are even commanded to use our kingdom authority to pray sincerely for those who persecute us—again, just as Christ did (Matt. 5:43–44; Luke 6:28). (Remember, he's talking to people who before long would be beheaded, burned alive, or fed to lions!) While people in the kingdom of the world usually do good to those who do good to them, followers of Jesus are called to do good even to those who harm them (Luke 6:34–35). When struck on the cheek, we are to offer up the other (Luke 6:29). When asked by an oppressive Roman guard to carry his equipment one mile, we are to offer to carry it two (Matt. 5:41).

Understood in their original context, these teachings do not tell us to allow people to abuse us, as though we are to love our enemies but not ourselves. To the contrary, Jesus is giving us a way by which we can keep from being defined by those who act unjustly toward us. When we respond to violence with violence, whether it be physical, verbal, or attitudinal, we legitimize the violence of our enemy and sink to his level. When we instead respond unexpectedly— offering our other cheek and going a second mile—we reveal, even as we expose the injustice of his actions, that our nemesis doesn't have the power to define us by those actions. In this sense we serve our enemy, for manifesting God's love and exposing evil (the two always go hand in hand) open up the possibility that he will repent and be transformed.[10]

Peter addressed this point when he spoke to a congregation about to undergo unjust persecution. "When [Jesus] was abused," Peter said, "he did not return abuse; when he suffered, he did not threaten; but he entrusted himself to the one who judges justly" (1 Peter 2:23). So when we are persecuted we are not to resort to violence (as Peter himself had done in the Garden!), but we are to "sanctify Christ as Lord" in our "hearts." In this way, he continues, we "put those who abuse [us] ... to shame" (1 Peter 3:16). Our refusal to sink to the level of our enemy opens up the possibility that the enemy will see the injustice of his treatment and perhaps be freed from his dehumanizing mindset.

Similarly, Paul says we are never to "repay anyone evil for evil" and "never avenge [ourselves]." All judgment is to be left to God (Rom. 12:17–19) who, among other things, uses governments to repay wrongdoers (Rom. 13:4). Instead, we who follow Jesus are to feed our enemy if they're hungry and give them water if they're thirsty. In this way, Paul says, we "will heap burning coals on their heads" (Rom. 12:20)—an idiomatic expression for bringing conviction on someone. Paul is saying that the stark contrast between an enemy's behavior and our loving response will bring conviction on them and possibly result in their transformation. This is how we keep our own heart from being "overcome by evil" and how we "overcome evil with good" (Rom. 12:21).

Whether we're talking about our response to a persecuting official, a threatening nation, or a mean-spirited coworker, kingdom people are to follow Jesus' example. This Calvary-like response to conflict and violence is only possible, however, if we allow the Spirit to purge our heart of "all bitterness and wrath and anger and wrangling and slander, together with all malice" (Eph. 4:31). If we follow the "pattern of this world" (Rom. 12:2 NIV) and allow bitterness and hatred into our heart, and if we consequently demonize our enemy, we cannot possibly obey Jesus' teaching—or Peter's and Paul's. For their teaching is not merely that we are to *act lovingly* toward our enemy while we clench our teeth. No, we are to *genuinely* love them, and one's ability and willingness to do this is the most distinctive manifestation of the reign of God in one's life.

Martin Luther King Jr. captured the heart of Jesus' ethic of loving one's enemy as he discussed the concept of nonviolent resistance advocated by Mahatma Gandhi (who himself was influenced by Christ's teachings). King wrote that the concept of *Satyagraha* (meaning "power of love and truth") "avoids not only external physical violence but also violence of spirit. The nonviolent resister not only refuses to shoot his opponent but he also refuses to hate him." Later, King commented, "Along the way of life, someone must have sense enough and morality enough to cut off the chain of hate. This can be done by projecting the ethic of love to the center of our lives."[11]

As Gandhi frequently noted, *Satyagraha* is more a discipline of will, mind, and emotions than behavior. When put into practice, however, loving one's enemies and returning evil with good has a power to accomplish something the kingdom of the sword can never dream of: namely, freeing the enemy from his hatred and stopping the ceaseless cycle of violence that hatred fuels.

Jesus' ethic is clearly predicated on people acquiring a love that participates in God's unconditional love for all, for apart from this love, his teachings are absurd. Just as God "is kind to the ungrateful and the wicked" (Luke 6:35), and just as God allows the blessings of nature to come "on the evil and on the good" (Matt. 5:45), Jesus says we are to love without consideration of others' moral status. We are to love as the sun shines and as the rain falls—in other words, indiscriminately. We are to "be merciful, just as [our] Father is merciful" (Luke 6:36). God's love is impartial and universal, unrestricted by typical kingdom-of-the-world familial, tribal, ethnic, and nationalistic loyalties, and so must ours be (Deut. 10:17–19; 2 Chron. 19:7; Mark 12:14; Acts 10:34; Rom. 2:10–11; Eph. 6:9; cf. 1 Tim. 2:4; 1 Peter 1:17; 2 Peter 3:9; 1 John 4:8). As we noted above, we are to consider *anyone* in need a "neighbor" whom we are called to serve (Luke 10:27–37). Consequently, we are to give to beggars and lend to those in need without expecting anything in return (Matt. 5:39–42; Luke 6:31–36). We are, in short, to love and serve without judgment, without condition, and without any consideration of what's in it for us.

If this teaching sounds impractical and irrational—to the point where we might want to come up with clever rationalizations to get around it—this is simply evidence of how much we have bought into the thinking of the kingdom of the world. By kingdom-of-the-world standards, this *is* impractical and irrational, for in kingdom-of-the-world thinking only "power over" is practical and rational. But this radical, non-common-sensical, "power under" love *is* the kingdom of God, for this loving way of living reflects the nature of God and looks like Jesus.

LIVING CONSISTENT WITH GOD'S CHARACTER

As Hauerwas and Willimon note, these radical teachings are not given as a "strategy for achieving a better society"—as though Jesus came to tweak the kingdom of the world. Rather:

They are an indication, a picture, a vision of the in-breaking of a new society. They are indicatives, promises, instances, imaginative examples of life in the kingdom of God....

THE KINGDOM OF THE CROSS / 43

[They] help us see something so new, so against what we have heard said, that we cannot rely on our older images of what is and what is not.[12]

What is more, while the kingdom of the world is centered on what "works" to achieve one's self-interests, Jesus' radical teachings are concerned with something entirely different, based on the character of God. Hauerwas and Willimon write:

> The basis for the ethics of the Sermon on the Mount is not what works but rather the way God is. Cheek-turning is not advocated as what works (it usually does not), but advocated because this is the way God is—God is kind to the ungrateful and the selfish. This is not a stratagem for getting what we want but the only manner of life available, now that, in Jesus, we have seen what God wants. We seek reconciliation with the neighbor, not because we feel so much better afterward, but because reconciliation is what God is doing in the world through Christ.[13]

This is simply who God is and what God is up to in the world, and so living consistent with God's character, reflected in the teachings of Jesus, is simply *what it means* to submit to God's reign. In sharp contrast to kingdom-of-the-world thinking, therefore, disciples of Jesus aren't to act first and foremost on the basis of what seems practical or effective at securing a good outcome. We are to act on the basis of what is *faithful* to the character and reign of God, trusting that, however things may appear in the short term, in the long run God will redeem the world with such acts of faithfulness.

God's reign is manifested and expanded through the faithfulness of his subjects, and so, where people choose peace over violence and forgiveness over retaliation, acting in the interest of others rather than out of self-interest, the kingdom of God is present. Where people choose violence, retaliation, and self-interest, however, they are merely participants in the kingdom of the world, however understandable or "justified" their behavior is by kingdom-of-the-world standards. The way of living under God's reign is shocking and impractical within the context of the kingdom of the world, but it is the only way that is in harmony with God, in concert with what he is doing in the world, and, thus, the only way that manifests his reign.[14]

THE ALL OR NOTHING OF LOVE

The rest of the New Testament confirms the centrality of Calvary-quality love for people who want to participate in the kingdom of God. Perhaps nowhere is this more powerfully communicated than in 1 Corinthians 13. Here Paul says:

> If I speak in the tongues of mortals and of angels, but do not have love, I am a noisy gong or a clanging cymbal. And if I have prophetic powers, and understand all mysteries and all knowledge, and if I have all faith, so as to remove mountains, but do not have love, I am nothing. If I give away all my possessions, and if I hand over my body so that I may boast, but do not have love, I gain nothing. (1 Cor. 13:1–3)

Listen carefully to what Paul is saying. A more radical teaching on love couldn't be imagined! Most of us could not help but be impressed by someone who could speak in a beautiful angelic tongue or who possessed powerful prophetic gifts. But these abilities amount to nothing more than religious noise—a clanging cymbal —unless motivated by love and used for the purpose of love. And who wouldn't be impressed by someone who understood all mysteries or possessed all knowledge? Yet if they don't use these marvelous gifts to "come under" others in love, they are altogether worthless. And who could criticize someone who had mountain-moving faith or who gave away all their possessions or even heroically sacrificed their life? Yet Paul says that if these aren't done for the purpose of loving others, they are devoid of value, at least from a kingdom-of-God perspective. They may be very impressive within the context of a religious version of the kingdom of the world, but they are utterly insignificant in the kingdom of God, except insofar as they manifest Calvary-like love.

The *only* criteria that matters, then, in assessing whether anything has any value within the kingdom that God is building on earth is love—love defined as Jesus dying on the cross for those who crucified him (1 John 3:16). However impressive a gift or achievement may be in its own right, it has no kingdom value except insofar as it manifests God's love—except insofar as it looks like Jesus Christ.

How might our churches be different if we took Paul's teaching seriously? What would happen if the ultimate criteria we used to assess how "successful" or "unsuccessful" our churches were was the question, *are we loving as Jesus loved?* The truth of the matter is that we are only carrying out God's will and expanding the kingdom of God to the extent that we answer *that* question affirmatively. No other question, criteria, or agenda can have any meaning for kingdom-of-God devotees except insofar as it helps us respond to *that* question.

The rest of the New Testament further confirms this teaching. Paul and Peter, following Jesus, teach that the distinguishing mark of a follower of Jesus is that they imitate Jesus in how they love (Eph. 5:1–2; 1 Peter 2:21). So too, throughout his first epistle the apostle John identifies love as the distinctive characteristic of God's children, for "God is love" (1 John 4:8). "We know that we have passed from death to life," John says, "because we love one another. Whoever does not love abides in death" (3:14). And again, "God is love, and those who abide in love abide in God, and God abides in them" (4:16; cf. 3:17; 4:7, 12, 21). What's most significant is that John defines the love he's talking about by pointing to Jesus Christ's sacrifice. It is *this* example we are called to follow (1 John 3:16).

Along these same lines, Paul teaches that everything we do is to be "done in love" (1 Cor. 16:14). As kingdom-of-God people, we should never engage in anything that is not motivated by Christlike love. We are to "live in love, as Christ loved us and gave himself up for us" (Eph. 5:2). "Above all," Paul says, "clothe yourselves with love ..." (Col. 3:14). Peter agrees when he writes, "Above all, maintain constant love for one another" (1 Peter 4:8). Nothing is to at any time be deemed more important to a kingdom disciple than "living in" and "clothing ourselves" with love—"as Christ loved us and gave himself up for us." It's not surprising, then, that so many of Paul's prayers for his congregations addressed their growth in Calvary-type love (Phil. 1:9; 1 Thess. 3:12; 2 Thess. 1:3).

THE CONTRAST OF THE TWO KINGDOMS

Once again, this is the kingdom of God: It looks and acts like Jesus Christ. It looks and acts like Calvary. It looks and acts like God's eternal, triune love. It consists of people graciously embracing others and sacrificing themselves in service to others. It consists of people trusting and employing "power under" rather than "power over," even when they, like Jesus, suffer because of this.[15] It consists of people imitating the Savior who died for them and for all people. It consists of people submitting to God's rule and doing his will. By definition, *this* is the domain in which God is king.

In this light, it should now be obvious why Jesus said his kingdom was "not from this world," for it contrasts with the kingdom of the world in every possible way. This is not a simple contrast between good and evil, for, as we've seen, God gives the governments of the kingdom of the world power to carry out the service of keeping law and order in a fallen world. Not only this, but kingdom-of-God citizens are to humbly acknowledge that we are the worst of sinners (Matt. 7:1–3; cf. 1 Tim. 1:15–16), acknowledging, as Jesus himself did (though he was sinless), that the only one who is truly good is God (Luke 18:19). The contrast is rather between two fundamentally different ways of doing life, two fundamentally different mindsets and belief systems, two fundamentally different loyalties.

It will be helpful to end this chapter by summarizing these contrasts under five headings.

- *A Contrast of Trusts:* The kingdom of the world trusts the power of the sword, while the kingdom of God trusts the power of the cross. The kingdom of the world advances by exercising "power over," while the kingdom of God advances by exercising "power under."
- *A Contrast of Aims:* The kingdom of the world seeks to control behavior, while the kingdom of God seeks to transform lives from the inside out. Also, the kingdom of the world is rooted in preserving, if not advancing, one's self-interests and one's own will, while the kingdom of God is centered exclusively on carrying out God's will, even if this requires sacrificing one's own interests. To experience the life of the kingdom of God, one has to die to self (Matt. 16:25; Mark 8:35; Luke 17:33; John 12:25; Gal. 2:19–20).
- *A Contrast of Scopes:* The kingdom of the world is intrinsically tribal in nature, and is heavily invested in defending, if not advancing, one's own people-group, one's nation, one's ethnicity, one's state, one's religion, one's ideologies, or one's political agendas. That is why it is a kingdom characterized by perpetual conflict. The kingdom of God, however, is intrinsically universal, for it is centered on simply loving as God loves. It is centered on people living for the sole purpose of replicating the love of Jesus Christ to all people at all times in all places without condition. The kingdom-of-God participant has by love transcended the tribal and nationalistic parameters of whatever version of the kingdom of the world they find themselves in.
- *A Contrast of Responses:* The kingdom of the world is intrinsically a tit-for-tat kingdom; its motto is "an eye for an eye and a tooth for a tooth." In this fallen world, no version of the kingdom of the world can survive for long by loving its enemies and blessing those who persecute it; it carries the sword, not the cross. But kingdom-of-God participants carry the cross, not the sword. We, thus, aren't ever to return evil with evil, violence with violence. We are rather to manifest the unique

kingdom life of Christ by returning evil with good, turning the other cheek, going the second mile, loving, and praying for our enemies. We are to respond to evil in a way that protects us from being defined by it and that exposes the evil as evil, thereby opening up the possibility that our "enemy" will be transformed. Far from seeking retaliation, we seek the well-being of our "enemy."

- *A Contrast of Battles:* The kingdom of the world has earthly enemies and, thus, fights earthly battles; the kingdom of God, however, by definition has no earthly enemies, for its disciples are committed to loving "their enemies," thereby treating them as friends, their "neighbors." There *is* a warfare the kingdom of God *is* involved in, but it is "not against enemies of blood and flesh." It is rather "against the rulers, against the authorities, against the cosmic powers of this present darkness, against the spiritual forces of evil in the heavenly places" (Eph. 6:12).

Conservative religious people involved in kingdom-of-the-world thinking often believe that their enemies are the liberals, the gay activists, the ACLU, the pro-choice advocates, the evolutionists, and so on. On the opposite side, liberal religious people often think that their enemies are the fundamentalists, the gay bashers, the Christian Coalition, the antiabortionists, and so on. Demonizing one's enemies is part of the tit-for-tat game of Babylon, for only by doing so can we justify our animosity, if not violence, toward them. What we have here are two different religious versions of the king-dom of the world going at each other. If we were thinking along the lines of the kingdom of God, however, we would realize that *none* of the people mentioned in the above lists are people whom king-dom-of-God citizens are called to fight *against*. They are, rather, people whom kingdom-of-God citizens are called to fight *for*.

Our battle is "not against flesh and blood," whether they are right wing or left wing, gay or straight, pro-choice or pro-life, lib-eral or conservative, democratic or communist, American or Iraqi. Our battle is against the "cosmic powers" that hold these people, and all people, in bondage. Whatever our own opinions about how the kingdom of the world should run, whatever political or ethical views we may happen to embrace, our one task as kingdom-of-God disciples is to fight *for* people, and the way we do it is by doing exactly what Jesus did. He defeated the cosmic powers of darkness by living a countercultural life characterized by outrageous love and by laying down his life for his enemies. So too, we contribute to the demise of the "power over" principalities that hold people in bondage when we refrain from judgment of others and rather extend grace to them, when we let go of anger toward others and instead "come under" them in loving service.

A person may win by kingdom-of-the-world standards but lose by the standards that eternally count—the standards of the kingdom of God. We can possess all the right kingdom-of-the-world opinions on the planet and stand for all the right kingdom-of-the-world causes, but if we don't look like Jesus Christ carrying his cross to Golgotha—sacrificing our time, energy, and resources for others—our rightness is merely religious noise. Jesus taught that there will be many who seem to believe right things and do religious deeds in his name whom he will renounce, for they didn't love him by loving the homeless, the hungry, the poor, and the prisoner (Matt. 7:21–23; 25:41–46; cf. Luke 6:46–49). However right we may be, without love we are simply displaying a religious version of the world, not the kingdom of God.

CHAPTER 3

KEEPING THE KINGDOM HOLY

Jesus concerns Himself hardly at all with the solution of worldly problems....
His word is not an answer to human questions and problems; it is the answer of God
to the question of God to man. His word is ... not a solution, but a redemption.

DIETRICH BONHOEFFER[1]

THE OBVIOUSNESS OF THE KINGDOM OF GOD

Though the word has come to mean a multitude of things these days (many of them negative), the word *Christian* originally suggested one who follows and looks like Christ. By definition, therefore, the distinctive mark of a Christian is that one aspires to think, feel, and act like Christ. "To be a disciple," Yoder notes, "is to share in that lifestyle of which the cross is the culmination."[2] Indeed, since Jesus is the incarnation of God, a Christian is one who, by definition, *imitates* God, as Paul says in Ephesians (5:1).

The Greek word for "imitate" (*mimetai*) literally means to "mimic" or to "shadow"—to do exactly what you see another doing, nothing more nor less. Thus, as disciples of Jesus we are to do what we see God doing in Jesus, just as our shadow does everything we do. Paul spells out what this shadowing looks like when he goes on to say: "Live in love, as Christ loved us and gave himself up for us" (Eph. 5:2). To be part of the body of Christ, to be a participant in the kingdom of God, means—by definition—that we mimic Jesus' love by how we live. We aren't to love just on occasion, when it's convenient, or when our enemies aren't attacking our nation. We are to *live* in this Calvary-quality love when we're breathing, when our brain is active, when our heart is beating. All we do is to be

51

done in love (1 Cor. 16:14), and insofar as we do this, we manifest the kingdom of God.

When the kingdom is manifested, it's rather obvious. It doesn't look like a church building. It doesn't necessarily look like a group of religious people professing certain things—including the profession that they are Christian. It doesn't necessarily look like a gathering of people advocating the right political or ethical causes. It doesn't look like a group who are—or who at least believe themselves to be—morally superior to others, telling them how they should live. It doesn't look like a group using swords, however righteous they believe their sword-wielding to be. It rather looks like people individually and collectively mimicking God. It looks like Calvary. It looks Christian, whether it identifies itself as such or not. When people are "coming under" others to love and serve them, without regard to how much or how little those others deserve it, and without regard for their own interests and reputation, the kingdom of God has come.

In a Homeric world filled with self-serving violence, this sort of love is not difficult to detect. People sometimes distinguish between the visible and invisible church as a way of distinguishing between the institutional church that is visible to all and the true body of disciples that only God can see. The distinction is valid if used to make the point that one can't assume they're a true disciple of Jesus just because they visibly associate with a church. But the distinction is not valid if it's meant to suggest that there's anything invisible about the kingdom of God—as though we can't know the extent to which an individual or institution is or is not manifesting the kingdom of God. For there's simply nothing invisible, or hidden, about the kingdom of God. It always looks like Jesus. The church is called to visibly manifest this kingdom. Indeed, this is why it's called "the body of Christ." As Eberhard Arnold notes:

> The fact that the church is the body of Christ means that Christ receives a body, a form or shape, and becomes visible and real in the world. Otherwise the word "body" is meaningless. And when theologians say that what is meant here

is the "invisible Christ," they are simply demonstrating the nonsense of which only theologians are capable.[3]

The kingdom of God is not an opaque concept, and when it's manifested, it's not an opaque reality. It always looks like Jesus, dying on Calvary for those who crucified him. It always has a servant quality to it, and in this fallen world in which individuals, social groups, and nations are driven by self-interest, this sort of radical, unconditional, and scandalous love is anything but invisible.

In seeing the kingdom, people see what God is like. No one can see God directly, John tells us, but in seeing our kingdom love for them, enacted in service, they see God's love manifested (1 John 4:12). By God's design and through the internal working of the Holy Spirit, this "seeing" is to convince them that Jesus Christ is the true revelation of the Father, if they are open to it (John 13:35; 17:20–26). By God's design, people are not to be won over to his kingdom primarily by our clever arguments, scary religious tracts, impressive programs, or our sheer insistence that they are going to hell unless they share our theological opinions. No, they are to be won over by the way in which we replicate Calvary to them. They are to *see* and *experience* the reality of the coming kingdom in us.

If we accepted the simple principle that the kingdom of God looks like Jesus, and if we were completely resolved that our sole business as kingdom-of-God citizens is to advance this kingdom by replicating Jesus' gracious love toward others, neither we nor the world would have to deliberate about where "the true church" is. Once we understand that the kingdom looks like Jesus, attracting tax collectors and prostitutes, serving the sick, the poor, and the oppressed, it is as obvious when it is present as it is when it is absent. There's nothing invisible about it.

PRESERVING THE HOLINESS

Nothing is more important to the cause of the kingdom of God than that we who are its subjects live out this Christlike vision of the kingdom. Which is to say, nothing is more important than that we keep the kingdom of God distinct from the kingdom of the world, both in our thought and in our action. We must keep the kingdom of God holy, which essentially means set apart, consecrated, or distinct. Only by doing so will we not be distracted from our sole task of living "in love, as Christ loved us and gave himself up for us."

Not everything about the kingdom of the world is bad. Insofar as versions of the kingdom of the world use their power of the sword to preserve and promote law, order, and justice, they are good. But the kingdom of the world, by definition, can never be the kingdom of God. It doesn't matter that we judge it good because it stands for the principles we deem important—"liberty and justice for all," for example. No version of the kingdom of the world, however comparatively good it may be, can protect its self-interests while loving its enemies, turning the other cheek, going the extra mile, or blessing those who persecute it. Yet loving our enemies and blessing those who persecute us is precisely what kingdom-of-God citizens are called to do. It's what it means to be Christian. By definition, therefore, you can no more have a Christian worldly government than you can have a Christian petunia or aardvark. A nation may have noble ideals and be committed to just principles, but it's not for this reason Christian.

The all-important distinction between the kingdom of God and the kingdom of the world entails that a kingdom-of-God citizen must take care never to align any particular version of the kingdom of the world with the kingdom of God. We may firmly believe one version to be better than another, but we must not conclude that this better version is therefore closer to the kingdom of God than the worse version. "The kingdom is not simply some cipher that we can fill in with our ideas about what a good society ought to look like," argues Hauerwas.[4] If we think in this fashion, we are comparing apples with oranges, and Calvary with petunias and aardvarks—and, as we shall later see, nothing but confusion and harm to *both* kingdoms ensue.

To be sure, a version of the kingdom of the world that effectively carries out law, order, and justice is indeed closer to God's will for *the kingdom of the world*. Decent, moral people should certainly encourage this as much as possible, whatever their religious faith might be. But no version of the kingdom of the world is closer to the kingdom of God than others because it does its job relatively well. For God's kingdom looks like Jesus, and no amount of sword-wielding, however just it may be, can ever get a person, government, nation, or world closer to that. The kingdom of God is not an ideal version of the kingdom of the world; it's not something that any version of the kingdom of the world can aspire toward or be measured against. The kingdom of God is a completely distinct, alternative way of doing life.

KEEPING A HEALTHY SUSPICION

In fact, far from aligning any version of the kingdom of the world with the kingdom of God, kingdom-of-God participants must retain a healthy suspicion toward every version of the kingdom of the world—especially their own (for here it is most tempting to become idolatrous). After all, on the authority of God's Word, we know that however good a particular government may be by world standards, it is nevertheless strongly influenced by fallen principalities and powers. Consequently, no kingdom-of-God citizen should ever place undue trust in any political ideology or program. Nor should they be overly shocked when kingdom-of-the-world leaders or parties act contrary to Christ's ways. The Roman officials of Jesus' day frequently behaved in grossly immoral ways, but neither Jesus nor any New Testament author exhibit any surprise or concern over this.[5] It was, it seems, par for the course for kingdom-of-the-world leaders in their view.

Not only this, but we know that however good a particular version of the kingdom of the world may be, it does not hold the ultimate answer to the world's problems. It may indeed be better in certain respects at maintaining law, order, and justice, for which we should be thankful. But the kingdom-of-God citizen knows that the world is not going to be fundamentally transformed by the "power over" use of the sword. We know that love, peace, and justice will not be experienced on a global scale until the kingdom of God is permanently established, until human nature is fundamentally transformed, and until the corrupting influence of demonic powers is finally destroyed. Take it on God's authority if it's not already obvious to you: the ultimate hope of the world lies not in human, kingdom-of-the-world wisdom, but in the advancement of God's kingdom and the return of Jesus Christ!

In fact, the kingdom-of-God citizen should know that, far from holding the ultimate answer to the world's problems, even the best versions of the kingdom of the world are part of the world's problem. The fundamental problem in the world is that fallen people trust "power over" rather than "power under," coercion rather than love. Because we are in bondage, we tend to preserve and promote our self-interests with force. Far from resisting (let alone transforming) this fallen tendency, even the best versions of the kingdom of the world have to capitalize on it.

Every version of the kingdom of the world defends itself and advances its cause by rallying the self-interest of its citizens into a collective tribal force that makes each citizen willing to kill and be killed for what it believes to be the good of the society. It survives and advances by uniting and motivating its subjects around their distinct collective identity, ideals, self-interest, and desire for security—over and against any individuals or governments whose own tribal identity, ideals, self-interest, and desire for security might impinge on or threaten their own. To this end, every version of the kingdom of the world demonizes its enemies when necessary to generate the motivation to go to war and to convince those who must spill blood that their cause is righteous.

It is this "us-them" mindset that makes conflict inevitable, as Homer clearly saw. So long as people are willing to advance their self-interest by force, and so long as their sense of identity, worth, and security is rooted in their national, ethnic, religious, or political distinctives (their "tribal identity")—there will be violence and injustice. Until the kingdom of God transforms the entire globe, conflict is inevitable. This is not in any way to suggest that kingdom-of-God people should not pray and strive for peace in the world, for we are called to be peacemakers (Matt. 5:9). Though we are not "of" the world, we *are* "in" it. But we must also remember that the essential problems of the world, including its inescapable tendency toward violent conflict, will not be finally resolved until human nature is fundamentally transformed by the global establishment of the kingdom of God.

Only when every knee bows and every tongue confesses the loving lordship of Christ (Phil. 2:10–11); only when Christ has transformed our hearts into his likeness (Rom. 8:29; 2 Cor. 3:18; 4:4; Phil. 3:21), and only when everything in heaven and on earth has been purged by the fire of God's loving judgment (2 Peter 3:7, 10, 12) will the fundamental problems of the world be eradicated. And the only way to move toward this goal is for kingdom-of-God citizens to exercise "power under" rather than "power over." It happens only as the mustard seed of the kingdom of God (cf. Matt. 13:31–32) grows through individual and corporate replications of Calvary.

JESUS IN POLITICALLY TROUBLED TIMES

Jesus' life and ministry consistently preserved the radical uniqueness of the kingdom he came to establish, and as those whose life mission is to mimic Jesus, we are called to do the same. It wasn't always easy for him, and it's never easy for us. Indeed, in the next chapter we shall see that preserving the distinctness of the kingdom of God has always been the most important and most difficult task for the church—as well as the task we have most consistently failed at.

To appreciate the importance of preserving this distinction, we need to understand that the Jewish world Jesus was born into was a political hotbed. There was constant political and cultural friction between the ruling Romans and their Jewish subjects, and most Jews

despised the fact that they, "the true people of God," were tyranni-
cally ruled by God-denying, immoral pagans. Most Jews longed for
the appearing of a political messiah, like David, who would, by military force and the supernatural assistance of God, restore Israel to its
glory days. They saw it as a profound insult both to themselves and
to their God that they weren't an independent, sovereign nation.

At the same time, first-century Jews were deeply divided over
how to respond. On one extreme were the zealots who believed
that Jews should take up arms against the Romans, initiate war, and
trust that God would intervene to give them victory. Their battle
cry was something like, "We must vanquish our enemies and take
Israel back for God." On the other extreme were the "conservatives"
who thought it best not to trouble the waters but rather cooperate
with the Roman government as much as possible. In between these
two extremes were a number of positions, distinguished from each
other by how they answered an assortment of questions regarding
how much or how little Jews should acquiesce to or resist their
Roman rulers.

Should Jews obey Roman laws, and if so, which ones? Should
they pay taxes to Caesar, thereby supporting his tyrannical regime?
Should they participate in the Roman army and help defend its
empire? Should they pledge their allegiance to their reigning government by paying homage to statues of emperors? Should they be
educated in Roman (Hellenistic) literature and by Roman teaching
methods? Should they participate in nationalistic festivities? How
much Roman culture could they accept or reject? The list of particular questions was almost endless.

Into this intensely politicized situation Jesus was born. And not
surprisingly, throughout his ministry people tried to get him to
weigh in on these issues. They were expecting a political messiah
who would answer their questions, solve their problems, and lib-
erate them. What they didn't understand—what even Jesus' own
disciples were slow to learn—was that Jesus hadn't come to answer
their kingdom-of-the-world questions or solve their kingdom-of-
the-world problems. As Bonhoeffer insightfully noted:

Jesus concerns Himself hardly at all with the solution of worldly problems. When He is asked to do so His answer is remarkably evasive.... Indeed, He scarcely ever replies to men's questions directly, but answers rather from a quite different plane. His word is not an answer to human questions and problems; it is the answer of God to the question of God to man. His word is essentially determined not from below but from above. It is not a solution, but a redemption.[6]

Jesus didn't come to give us the Christian answer to the world's many sociopolitical quandaries, and he didn't come to usher in a new and improved version of the kingdom of the world. His agenda was far more radical, for he came to redeem the world and ultimately overthrow the kingdom of the world by ushering in an alternative kingdom. He came not to give solutions, tweak external regulations, and enforce better behavior. He rather came to transform lives from the inside out by winning people over to the reign of God's sovereign love, thereby rendering the "power over" tactics of the kingdom of the world unnecessary.

In the words of Andre Trocme, "Jesus came to bring a revolution, one that would impact every sphere of existence, including social and power relations.... He did not want to reform political structures but wanted everything to come under God's rulership."[7] Echoing that idea, Lee Camp writes:

Rather than accepting the existing social institutions as they stood, and reforming them from within; rather than seeking to establish top-down control and then dominate the masses; rather than propagating a merely "spiritual" message, Jesus instead set about to proclaim and embody a new order, the new Kingdom. And so he called disciples to join him in the endeavor.[8]

Jesus' mission wasn't to improve the old; his mission, and the mission he gave his disciples, was to embody the new—an entirely new way of doing life. It is life lived within the reign of God; life centered on God as the sole source of one's security, worth, and significance; life lived free from self-protective fear; and life manifested in Calvary-like service to others. His promise is that as his disciples manifest the unique beauty and power of this life, it will slowly and inconspicuously—like a mustard seed—grow and take over the garden.

GIVING TO GOD WHAT BELONGS TO GOD

Given how politicized his environment was, it is nothing short of amazing how thoroughly Jesus preserved the distinctness of the kingdom he came to bring. He refused to allow his unique kingdom to be co-opted by the kingdom of the world. He refused to let people's political and ethical concerns set his agenda. Instead, he wisely transformed every encounter into an opportunity to advance the kingdom of God.

For example, at several points in his ministry some of Jesus' opponents tried to entrap him in one of the hottest political topics of the day—the issue of paying taxes. They desperately wanted to thin out the crowd that was following him, and they knew that whatever side Jesus aligned himself with on this debate, he would alienate many in the crowd who held a different political opinion. But Jesus never bit the bait. Rather, he always found a way to move the discussion to a deeper level—a kingdom-of-God level.

In one instance, Jesus responded to the question of whether Jews should pay taxes or not by holding up a coin and asking, "Whose head is this, and whose title?" It was, of course, the emperor's. Jesus concluded, "Give ... to the emperor the things that are the emperor's, and [give] to God the things that are God's" (Matt. 22:20–22).

To grasp the ironic brilliance of Jesus' response, it's helpful to know that the Jews of this time were deeply offended by currency that bore the image of the emperor. They saw it not only as egotistical on the part of the emperor but also as a direct violation of the commandment against making images (Ex. 20:4; Lev. 26:1).[9] Only

God can make an image of himself, and he did so when he made humans (Gen. 1:26–27).

Jesus ingeniously linked the issue of pagan egotism and idolatry with the issue of paying taxes. With a tinge of sarcasm (I imagine Jesus with a wry smile giving this illustration), Jesus was in essence saying, "You of course believe this coin is an egotistical and idolatrous offense to God. So why should we who are God's people fight with each other over how much of *this* we should keep or give back to the egotistical, idol-making offenders?" The thing people should rather be concerned with, Jesus is saying, is whether or not they are giving to God what bears *his* image and what therefore belongs wholly to him—namely, their very lives. Indeed, Jesus was ironically suggesting that an inappropriate preoccupation with what we should do with Caesar's image may reflect a heart that is insufficiently preoccupied with what should be done with God's image. Even if someone comes up with the "correct" position on paying taxes (is there one?), what good does it do her if she loses her soul (Mark 8:36)?

In this way Jesus wisely used the kingdom-of-the-world issue with its limited and divisive kingdom-of-the-world options as a springboard to pose the kingdom-of-God question and the kingdom-of-God option. He was demonstrating, once again, that he hadn't come to resolve the ambiguous and controversial issues that characterize the kingdom of the world. He rather came to offer all a radical alternative way of doing life, answering a completely different set of questions concerned with living under the reign of God.

GUARDING AGAINST GREED

The same sort of wisdom is manifested in Jesus' response to the man who wanted him to settle a family matter. The man said to Jesus, "Teacher, tell my brother to divide the family inheritance with me" (Luke 12:13). The man apparently was feeling cheated by the governing Jewish law that gave the eldest son the right to disperse the family's inheritance, and he wanted Jesus to do something about it. He wanted him to use his public clout to force his brother to share, but Jesus refused to resolve his dilemma.

"Friend," Jesus said, "who set me to be a judge or arbitrator over you?" (Luke 12:14). He was in essence asking, "Do I *look* like your lawyer?" Jesus would not act as this man's legal counselor or his brother's ethical advisor, for these roles and issues lay outside the singular reason Jesus came to earth.

There was something, however, that was within the domain of Jesus' mission, and Jesus used the man's question as a springboard to address it. "Take care!" he told the man while the crowd listened. "Be on your guard against all kinds of greed; for one's life does not consist in the abundance of possessions" (Luke 12:15). However we resolve our ambiguous legal and ethical issues, Jesus was saying, the important thing is our heart and motives. For even if a person succeeds in improving the legal system and resolving particular ethical quagmires, it matters nothing if they continue to think that life consists in the abundance of possessions.

What Jesus offered this man, and what he came to offer all people, was a relationship with God that would free them from the need to fill the emptiness in their lives with things—whether material possessions, "right" ethical opinions, or righteous obedience to religious laws. Through Jesus, our life can be filled with a divine love, which alone satisfies the hunger of our soul. Only when the soul is filled can it be set free from the secular, ethical, and religious cravings that keep it in bondage.

CONSERVATIVES AND LIBERALS WITHIN THE SAME KINGDOM

Jesus would simply not allow the world to set the terms of his engagement with the world. This explains how (and perhaps *why*) he could call Matthew, a tax collector, as well as Simon, a zealot, to be his disciples (Matt. 10:3–4). Tax collectors were on the farthest right wing of Jewish politics, zealots on the farthest left wing. To compare them to, say, Ralph Nader and Rush Limbaugh wouldn't come close. In fact, historical records indicate that the zealots despised tax collectors even more than they despised the Romans, for tax collectors not only paid taxes to support the Roman government (something zealots deplored), but they actually made their living collecting taxes from other Jews on Rome's behalf. Even worse, tax collectors often enhanced their income by charging more than was due and keeping the difference. For this reason, zealots sometimes assassinated tax collectors!

Yet Matthew and Simon spent three years together ministering alongside Jesus. No doubt they had some interesting fireside chats about politics. But what is positively amazing is that they ministered together with Jesus to advance the kingdom of God. Just as interesting, we never find a word in the Gospels about their different political opinions. Indeed, we never read a word about what Jesus thought about their radically different kingdom-of-the-world views.

What this silence suggests is that, in following Jesus, Matthew and Simon had something in common that dwarfed their individual political differences in significance, as extreme as these differences were. This silence points to the all-important distinctness of the kingdom of God from every version of the kingdom of the world. To be sure, Jesus' life and teachings would undoubtedly transform the trust both had in their political views if they would allow it. At the very least, as the reign of God took hold in their lives, the tax collector would no longer cheat his clients and the zealot no longer kill his opponents. Yet Jesus invited them both to follow him *as they were*, prior to their transformation, and their widely divergent political views were never a point of contention with Jesus.

What are we to make, then, of the fact that the evangelical church is largely divided along political lines? The Christian position is declared to be Matthew's among conservatives, Simon's among liberals. While Jesus never sided with any of the limited and divisive kingdom-of-the-world options routinely set before him, the church today, by and large, swallows them hook, line, and sinker. Indeed, in some circles, whether conservative or liberal, taking particular public stands on social, ethical, and political issues, and siding with particular political or social ideologies, is the litmus test of one's orthodoxy. In many quarters, individuals and groups with different opinions about which version of the kingdom of the world is best don't have friendly fireside chats. If they communicate at all, it's shouting across picket lines![10]

What this suggests is that the church has been co-opted by the world. To a large degree, we've lost our distinct kingdom-of-God vision and abandoned our mission. We've allowed the world to define us, set our agenda, and define the terms of our engagement with it. We've accepted the limited and divisive kingdom-of-the-world options and therefore mirror the kingdom-of-the-world conflicts. Because of this, we have not sought wisdom from above (James 3:17), the wisdom Jesus consistently displayed that would help us discern a unique kingdom-of-God approach to issues to empower our moving beyond the stalemates and tit-for-tat conflicts that characterize the kingdom of the world. Instead, we've made these conflicts our own as we fight with each other over "the Christian" option.

We have lost the simplicity of the kingdom of God and have largely forsaken the difficult challenge of living out the kingdom. We have forgotten, if ever we were taught, the simple principle that the kingdom of God looks like Jesus and that our sole task as kingdom people is to mimic the love he revealed on Calvary. We have to a large degree gone AWOL on the kingdom of God, allowing it to be reduced to a religious version of the world. The world supplies the options, and in direct contradiction to Jesus' example, we think it's our job to pronounce which one God thinks is right.

A DIFFICULT SIMPLICITY

Our central job is not to solve the world's problems. Our job is to draw our entire life from Christ and manifest that life to others. Nothing could be simpler—and nothing could be more challenging. Perhaps this partly explains why we have allowed ourselves to be so thoroughly co-opted by the world. It's hard to communicate to a prostitute her unsurpassable worth by taking up a cross for her, serving her for years, gradually changing her on the inside, and slowly winning the trust to speak into her life (*and* letting her speak into *our* life, for we too are sinners). Indeed, this sort of Calvary-like love requires one to die to self. It is much easier, and more gratifying, to assume a morally superior stance and feel good about doing our Christian duty to vote against "the sin of prostitution." Perhaps this explains why many evangelicals spend more time fighting against certain sinners in the political arena than they do sacrificing for those sinners. But Jesus calls us and empowers us to follow his example by taking the more difficult, less obvious, much slower, and more painful road—the Calvary road. It is the road of self-sacrificial love.

When we adopt this distinct kingdom-of-God stance, everything changes. While living in the kingdom of the world, of course, we still wrestle with tax and inheritance issues. And we should do so as decently and as effectively as possible. But our unique calling as kingdom people is not to come up with God's opinion of the right solution to these issues. Our unique calling is simply to replicate Christ's sacrificial love in service to the world.

When we return to the simplicity and difficulty of the kingdom of God, the question that defines us is no longer, What are the Christian policies and candidates? No, when love is placed above all kingdom-of-the-world concerns (Col. 3:14; 1 Peter 4:8), the kingdom-of-the-world options placed before us dwindle in significance—as much as Matthew's and Simon's fireside opinions were dwarfed in significance by their common allegiance to Jesus. For we, like Matthew and Simon know that the one question we are commanded to wrestle with is this: How do we love like Christ loves? Or to ask the same question in different ways: How do we communicate to others the unsurpassable worth they have before God? How can we individually and collectively serve in this particular context? How can we "come under" people here and now? How can we demonstrate Calvary love to every person? The revolution Jesus came to bring was "a genuinely human one," as Andre Trocme notes. "People, not principles, were his concern."[11]

We need not be able to figure out how society should tax its citizens, enforce inheritance laws, or deal with prostitutes. Neither Jesus, nor Paul, nor any New Testament author gave inspired pronouncements about such matters. But that does not prevent us from washing the feet of overly taxed citizens, disgruntled younger brothers, and despised prostitutes. Jesus and the New Testament authors gave plenty of inspired pronouncements about that.

CHAPTER 4

From RESIDENT ALIENS to CONQUERING WARLORDS

Therefore come out from them, and be separate from them, says the Lord ...
and I will be your father, and you shall be my sons and daughters,
says the Lord Almighty.

2 CORINTHIANS 6:17–18

You've got to kill the terrorists before the killing stops.
And I'm for the president to chase them all over the world.
If it takes ten years, blow them all away in the name of the Lord.

JERRY FALWELL[1]

BEING THE FIRST FRUITS

According to the biblical narrative and church tradition, at some point in the primordial past, Satan managed to deceive humanity and co-opt us into his rebellion against God, seizing the world and making humanity his slaves. Jesus came into this world not only to take it back and free earth's inhabitants but also to put an end to the war altogether. He came to destroy the Devil and his works (1 John 3:8; cf. Heb. 2:14). In becoming a human, the Son of God was entering "enemy-occupied territory," as C. S. Lewis says—the territory in which Satan was "ruler" and "god" (John 12:31; 2 Cor. 4:4).[2]

Now, through his death and resurrection, Jesus accomplished the task for which he came. He defeated the kingdom of darkness and set humanity free. In principle, therefore, the world has already been reconciled to God (2 Cor. 5:14–21; Col. 1:15–20). In principle, the wall of sin that separates humanity along ethnic, cultural, socioeconomic, and tribal lines has been destroyed. In principle, all have already died in Adam and been made alive in Christ (1 Cor. 15:22; 2 Cor. 5:14). In principle, we are already one new humanity in Christ (Eph. 2:14–15). *In principle*. Yet Scripture as well as our own experience make it painfully clear that what is true in principle has not yet been manifested as accomplished fact (see, for example, Heb. 2:8).[3]

From God's eternal perspective, the interval between what is true in principle and what is manifested as fact is undoubtedly no larger than the interval we experience between, say, turning on a light switch, on the one hand, and seeing the room completely filled with light, on the other. From *our* perspective, however, the interval has already lasted two thousand years, and for all we know may go on for another ten thousand (popular apocalyptic authors notwithstanding!) (2 Peter 3:8).

Now, we need to understand that this interval is not to be a time in which we passively wait for the end. Rather, it is the time in which the kingdom of God that was planted at Calvary is supposed to grow in us and through us to encompass the entire world. People who are submitted to the King, and whose lives are therefore being transformed into a domain in which God reigns, are called the "first fruits" of God, because they manifest in their lives what humanity and the world will look like when God's kingdom is fully manifested (2 Thess. 2:13; James 1:18; Rev. 14:4). We are to show ahead of time the eschatological harvest that is coming; we are to reveal the future in the present, the "already" amid the "not yet."

What is more, the Calvary-quality beauty of this coming kingdom revealed in our lives is to be the primary means by which the mustard-seed kingdom expands in the world. Tax collectors, prostitutes, and all others who hunger for real life are drawn to the beauty of the kingdom of Jesus, who was *the* first fruit of the new humanity (Rom. 8:29; Col. 1:18).

To be these first fruits, we must allow the kingdom to grow in us and through us. When we genuinely repent (turn from) our idolatrous allegiances to the world and submit to God's loving rule, the kingdom gets planted in our innermost being. From there, as the Holy Spirit continually teaches us to yield, the kingdom slowly takes over our hearts, minds, and finally, our behavior. As we learn to think, feel, and act under God's rule, we learn how to get our worth, significance, and security from Christ alone. We learn how to be freed from our addiction to futilely trying to acquire worth, significance, and security for ourselves. We learn how to walk in freedom from violence, self-centeredness, materialism, nationalism, racism, and all other false ways of getting life. As we die to our old self and "put on" our "new self" created in Christ Jesus (Eph. 4:22–24), we learn how to be loved and how to love God, ourselves, our neighbor, our enemies, as well as the animal kingdom and the earth God originally placed under our dominion and loving care (Gen. 1:28–30).

As we grow in Christlikeness, we grow as conduits of the kingdom, increasingly manifesting the fact that we are "first fruits." Through our Christlike love, others are brought under the influence of the kingdom until, in time, it is planted in them and the process taking place in us begins to take place in them. This is how the mustard seed takes over the entire garden (Matt. 13:31–32); this is how demonic powers are defeated. And this is how what is true in principle becomes manifested as fact.

STATIONED BEHIND ENEMY LINES

We play an important role in this momentary interval between Calvary and the full manifestation of the kingdom of God on earth. We are not only the garden that is taken over by the mustard seed; we are the means by which the mustard seed continues to take over the rest of the garden! God wants to work with us to grow his kingdom; indeed, the sovereign God chooses to need us to grow his kingdom.[4] He longs for a bride who learns how to rule with him upon the earth (2 Tim. 2:12; Rev. 5:10; 20:6; 22:5). Hence, things genuinely hang upon whether or not we fully yield to the kingdom growing in us and through us. While we are loved unconditionally, we are only as useful to the kingdom as we are yielded.

As yielded vessels, we are to do what Jesus did. Indeed, to the extent that we are yielded, Jesus himself continues to act through us as we saw in chapter 2. But by the same means, the enemy that confronted Jesus in his earthly ministry continues to confront him through us as we work with God to advance his kingdom. Though God's archenemy was in principle defeated on Calvary, this is not yet manifested fact, and so we continue to live in the war-torn interval between the "already" and the "not yet."

This is why Scripture makes it clear that, even after the resurrection of Christ, Satan is still the god of this age, the ruler of the power of the air, the highest functional ruler on the planet who controls the entire world, and the one who still opposes the advancement of the kingdom at every turn.[5] This means that all who have the kingdom of God growing in them must understand that they are stationed "behind enemy lines" as much as Jesus was. The world is still "enemy-occupied territory." The "pattern of this world" is still demonically structured, and so we must still resist being conformed to it (Rom. 12:2 NIV). We who have Christ being formed within us are no more at home in this present world system than Jesus himself was, and so our attitude toward the present world system must be the same as his. His kingdom was not of this world, and we who are part of this kingdom must never forget that *we* are not of this world either (John 17:16; cf. 8:23; 15:18–19; 17:14).

THE CALL TO BE "HOLY" RESIDENT ALIENS

Scripture drives home this truth when it teaches that we are to view ourselves as soldiers stationed in a foreign country and, thus, are not to let ourselves get overly entangled in "civilian affairs" (2 Tim. 2:4). It tells us that we are to see ourselves as aliens and exiles in a foreign country, just as Abraham did (Heb. 11:8–10, 13–16; 1 Peter 2:11). Whatever country we may naturally belong to, Paul says, we are to remember always that our real citizenship is in heaven (cf. Phil. 3:20). Whatever opinions we have about how to solve society's problems, we are to remember always that we cannot serve two masters (Luke 16:13). Our allegiance, therefore, can never be to any version of the kingdom-of-the-world, however much better we may think it is than other versions of the kingdom-of-the-world. Our allegiance is to our heavenly Father, whose country we belong to and into whose family we've been adopted (Rom. 8:29; Gal. 1:2; 6:10; Eph. 1:4–5).

Stanley Hauerwas and William Willimon capture the unique nature of the true church when they depict it as a small colony in a foreign land, "an island of one culture in the middle of another."[6] As the title of their masterful book denotes, we are to see ourselves as "resident aliens." We are *in* the world, but are not *of* the world any more than Jesus was of the world (John 17:16); we are to march to the beat of a different drummer. And—note this carefully—preserving this "alien status" is not an addendum to our calling as kingdom-of-God citizens; it belongs to the essence of what it means to be a kingdom-of-God citizen. The way we advance the kingdom of God is by being the unique kingdom of God in contrast to the kingdom of the world.

This is why Scripture repeatedly stresses the fact that we are called to be a "holy" people (2 Cor. 6:17), a concept that indicates something consecrated and set apart (Ps. 4:3). Like the Israelites coming out of Egypt, we are to come out from the world and be "set apart" for God. We utterly trivialize this profound biblical teaching if we associate our peculiar holiness with a pet list of religious taboos (such as smoking, drinking, dancing, gambling, and so on). No, the holiness the New Testament is concerned with is centered on being Christlike, living in outrageous, self-sacrificial love. If you make this your life aspiration, you will certainly be peculiar—about as peculiar as a Messiah dying on a cursed tree! You will be a "resident alien."

AVOIDING UNBIBLICAL DISTORTIONS

It's important that we understand that the primary reason God called Israel to be a holy nation was not to isolate it from other nations but to raise it up *for* other nations. Israel was to serve other nations by being their light, winning the world over to allegiance to Yahweh (e.g., Isa. 49:6; 55:4–5; 60:3–5; Jer. 3:17; Zech. 2:11; 8:20–23; cf. 1 Peter 2:9). God's plan was always to bless the entire world through Israel (e.g., Gen. 12:2–3; 17:4–6; 18:18; Ezek. 36:23; 37:28), and he has always been the God of all the nations (e.g., Ps. 46:10; 47:8; 67:2, 4; 72:11), working toward a kingdom that would include all people (Isa. 45:23; Acts 17:24–28; Rom. 14:11; Phil. 2:10–11; Rev. 5:9; 7:9; 14:6). So too, the reason God now calls kingdom people to remain separate from the ways of the kingdom-of-the-world is not to isolate them from their culture but to empower them to authentically serve their culture and ultimately win it over to allegiance to Jesus Christ. The reason we are not to be *of* the world is so we may be *for* the world.

This point is especially important today, for a significant portion of evangelical Christianity has come under the influence of an escapist apocalyptic theology. Believing Jesus will soon "rapture" Christians out of the world before destroying it, they have little concern with the church being a witness on issues of social justice, global peace, the environment, and so on. To the contrary, in the name of fulfilling biblical prophecy, many are actively supporting stances that directly or indirectly encourage violence, possibly on a global scale (for instance, extremist Christian Zionism). Since the world is doomed for soon destruction, the thinking goes, the only thing that matters is getting individuals ready for the rapture.[7]

Whatever else one thinks about the New Testament's eschatology, it certainly does not encourage this sort of irresponsible escapism. The hope offered to believers is not that we will be a peculiar elite group of people who will escape out of the world, leaving others behind to experience the wrath of God. The hope is rather that by our sacrificial participation in the ever-expanding kingdom, the whole creation will be redeemed (Rom. 8:20–23; Col. 1:18–20). God so loved *the world* he sent his Son (John 3:16), and we are to so love *the world* that we are willing to imitate this sacrificial behavior (Eph. 5:1–2). If we do this, we will certainly be a "peculiar" people. But following the example of Jesus, our peculiarity will lie in our willingness to incarnate ourselves in the tribulations of the world, not in possessing a "rapture ticket" that allows us to escape the tribulations of the world.

The holiness of the kingdom of God is its peculiar love, distinct from everything in the world. It is the unique mark of kingdom citizenship and constitutes our distinct witness to the world (John 13:35; 17:20–26; 1 John 3:14; 4:8–12). Hence, everything hangs on preserving this holiness and resisting the Devil's ongoing temptation to compromise it by reducing the kingdom of God to a religious version of the kingdom of the world.

THE TEMPTATION TO DO "GOOD"

Paul says we must not be ignorant of Satan's schemes, for they are subtle (2 Cor. 2:11). We thus need to explore the nature of the temptation Jesus faced—and consequently, the temptation we also face—as we seek to live out the holiness of the kingdom of God.

The Devil tempted Jesus by offering him all the kingdoms of the world without having to go to the cross (Luke 4:6–8). In essence, the Devil was offering him the very thing he came to get, for Jesus came for the people of the world, and people are always subjects of some kingdom or other. To rule the people, all Jesus had to do was submit to the "power over" god of this age and leave him in place as its ruling authority.

Think about this. Without having to suffer and die, Jesus could have immediately taken a position as the functional lord of all these kingdoms. True, Satan would have remained over him. His rule, therefore, would have had to participate in the "system of domination" that runs the world.[8] But at the very least, Jesus' position of power would have made the world a whole lot better. He could have quickly overpowered evil in all societies. He could have immediately alleviated much, if not all, suffering and created a kingdom of the world that enacted perfect law, order, and justice. Not only this, but he would have thereby fulfilled all his people's expectations of what a messiah was supposed to be and freed Israel from the tyranny of the Romans. Those he loved (and he loved all) could have experienced an immediate, vast improvement in their lives. The Devil's temptation would not have been a genuine temptation for Jesus unless there was a lot of "good" wrapped up in it.

Yet Jesus refused. Why? Because Jesus didn't come to make the kingdom-of-the-world a new and improved version of itself, let alone a Christian version of itself. Instead, he came to transform "the kingdom of the world" into "the kingdom of our Lord and of his Messiah" and thereby establish the rule of God, in place of the Devil, "forever and ever" (Rev. 11:15). He came to ultimately put the kingdom of the world out of business by establishing a counter-kingdom of radical love that would eventually render it obsolete.

As tempting as it was, Jesus was not going to allow the radical distinctness of the kingdom of God to be co-opted by the demoni-cally ruled kingdom of the world—however good the immediate consequences may have been. He was not going to trade in his holy mission—his radically peculiar mission—for a good kingdom-of-the-world mission. He was not going to do the practical thing and win the world by acquiring "power over" nations. He was, rather, going to win the world by exhibiting "power under" nations. He didn't want the authority of the world's kingdom that the Devil was offering him; he wanted only to exercise the unique authority his Father had given him. Hence, in obedience to the reign of his Father, Jesus took the impractical, slow, discrete, and self-crucifying road to transforming the world.

This wasn't just an unavoidable means to a noble end. To the con-trary, this act of love in obedience to the Father expresses the very heart of the kingdom that Jesus came to establish. "The cross is not a detour or a hurdle on the way to the kingdom," Yoder correctly notes, "it *is* the kingdom come."[9] Sacrificial love, therefore, isn't sim-ply an effective means to a greater good: it *is* the "set apart" kingdom of God on earth! When one obeys God and loves as Christ loves in a kingdom-of-the-world context, it always looks like this. This is the "holiness"—the set-apartness—of God's kingdom on earth. And this is why everything hangs on not allowing it to become co-opted by immediate, obvious, and self-serving kingdom-of-the-world methods, however good the immediate consequences may appear to be.[10]

Jesus knew what we must know: Everything rests on our resisting the Devil's temptation to do what seems to be immediate good things without suffering, instead of kingdom-of-God things that are slow, discrete, and always involve an element of sacrifice. As Camp argues, everything hangs on our confidence that

> it is not through the power brokers of human history that God will effect God's purposes, but through the little minority band of peoples committed to walking in the way of Jesus of Nazareth, bearing witness to the new reality, the new creation, the kingdom of God.

But as Camp further notes, this requires "great trust: that it is not our task to make things turn out right, but instead to be faithful witnesses. We have to trust that God will be God, and do what God has promised."[11]

THE CHURCH MILITANT AND TRIUMPHANT

Tragically, the history of the church has been largely a history of believers refusing to trust the way of the crucified Nazarene and instead giving in to the very temptation he resisted. It's the history of an institution that has frequently traded its holy mission for what it thought was a good mission. It is the history of an organization that has frequently forsaken the slow, discrete, nonviolent, sacrificial way of transforming the world for the immediate, obvious, practical, and less costly way of improving the world. It is a history of a people who too often identified the kingdom of God with a "Christian" version of the kingdom of the world.

For the first three hundred years, this wasn't so. Followers of Jesus during this time saw themselves as "resident aliens." They were a persecuted minority and as such did not dream of corporately exercising "power over" others. Indeed, the church of this time grew—and grew at a mind-boggling rate! This growth came about not by Christians fighting for their rights, as so many do today, but largely by Christians being put to death! It was during this time that the word *martyr,* which originally meant "witness," came to mean "one who dies for their faith," for dying was one of the primary ways these early Christians witnessed for their faith. In fact, many considered it an honor to be allowed to imitate Christ in being sacrificed for the kingdom they were citizens of.

This is not to suggest that the early church was a perfect expression of the kingdom of God; they had their all-too-human faults as we all do and absorbed their share of pagan ideas and attitudes. But as a corporate whole, their general relationship with the kingdom of the world replicated that of Jesus. To a large degree, the early church looked like a corporate version of Jesus dying on the cross for those who crucified him. The main proof they offered the world that Jesus was real was the fact that the new reality of the kingdom was manifested in their lives, both individually and corporately.[12]

It's difficult to overemphasize the change that occurred when, in AD 312, the emperor Constantine was converted. Just prior to an important battle, legend has it that Constantine had a vision in which he was told to paint Chi Rho (the first two letters of the Greek word for "Christ") on the shields of his soldiers. Allegedly, a voice in the vision announced, "By this sign you shall conquer." Constantine obeyed the vision and won the battle. The magic apparently worked, and so Constantine and his administration dedicated themselves to the Christians' God. This was the first time anyone ever associated the Christian faith with violence, but its success stained the church from then on.

Constantine legalized Christianity in AD 313, and because of its association with him, the religion immediately exploded in popularity. Within seventy years it was proclaimed the official religion of the Roman empire—making it a crime *not* to be a Christian (the Jews were exempt from the law, but not from the growing anti-Semitism of the church). The first recorded instance of Christians killing pagans occurred shortly after. In short order, the militant church extended its power by conquering lands and peoples throughout Europe, compelling them to become baptized Christians or die. As Charlemagne instructed his Christian troops in their conquest of the Saxons: "If there is anyone of the Saxon people lurking among them unbaptized, and if he scorns to come to baptism ... and stay a pagan, let him die."[13]

The "power under" kingdom centered on the cross had succeeded in becoming a massive "power over" kingdom centered on the sword. The church had become "the church militant and triumphant," and the kingdom of God, manifested in the crucified Nazarene, had become the empire of Christendom.

The sacrificial love and humility that characterized Christ and the early church had to be reinterpreted at this time to accommodate the new power that church leaders believed God had given to the church. Instead of being seen as the essence of the kingdom of God, the "power under" lifestyle of Jesus and the early Christians came to be understood as a provisional inconvenience that had to be tolerated until Christianity could gain status in the world. Jesus and the early disciples *had* to be humble and suffer, it was argued, because they didn't have the power to do otherwise. Forgetting that "the god of this age" owns all the authority of the kingdom of the world and gives it to whoever he wills (Luke 4:6–8), church leaders of this time insisted that God had given the church the power of the sword and thus concluded the church had an obligation to use it.

Indeed, since the church knows the truth and thus knows what is best for all people, the thinking generally went, it would be positively immoral to lay this power aside and "come under" the heathen. Rather, for their sake and for the glory of God, the church must use its newfound "power over" to compel (by force) heathens and heretics to agree with it and be saved. Why else would God have given this power to us, they thought?

A HISTORY OF PERSECUTION IN JESUS' NAME

What followed was a long and terrible history of people using the sword "in Jesus' name for the glory of God." Though there are, of course, many wonderful examples of Christlike people and movements throughout church history, the reigning church as a whole—"Christendom"—acted about as badly as most versions of the kingdom of the world. The Holy Roman Empire was about as violent as the Roman Empire it aspired to replace. It just carried out its typical kingdom-of-the-world barbarism under a different banner and in service to a different god.

Augustine was the first theologian to align the church in an official way with the use of the sword, and it happened to be against a fellow Christian group, the Donatists. Among other things, the Donatists believed that the alliance between the church and the state that had been forged since Constantine was undermining the purity and integrity of the church, and they wanted to keep the church pure.[14] Though Augustine had previously spoken against the use of coercion for religious purposes, his ongoing battle with the Donatists led him to reverse his view.

Augustine now justified the use of force by arguing that inflicting temporal pain to help someone avoid eternal pain is justified. Since God had given the church the power of the sword, Augustine reasoned, it had a responsibility to use it to further God's purposes in the world just as a stern father has a responsibility to beat his child for his own good. Since God sometimes uses terror for the good of humans, we who are God's representatives on earth—the church—may use terror for the sake of the gospel.[15] If the end justifies it, the use of violence as a means to that end is justified. (This is, in essence, Augustine's "just war" policy.) Augustine thus invoked a recent edict of the emperor Theodosius to criminalize the "heresy" of Donatism and attempt to persecute it out of existence. This set a tragic precedent for handling doctrinal disagreements for the next thirteen hundred years.

Throughout the Middle Ages and into the Renaissance, millions were burned at the stake, hung, beheaded, or executed in other ways for resisting some aspect of the church's teaching or for failing to operate under its authority.[16] Thousands upon thousands were tortured in unthinkable ways in an attempt to elicit a confession of faith in the Savior and the church; some of the macabre torturing devices were even inscribed with the logo "Glory be only to God." Christian sectarian groups such as the Paulicans, Cathars, Albigensians, and Waldensians were massacred by the towns—often including women and children—and Christians in both the West and the East slaughtered each other in Jesus' name as ruthlessly as they slaughtered Muslims. Terrible atrocities were carried out on Jews, especially when the Crusades needed to be financed, and multitudes of women (estimates range between sixty thousand to several million) were burned or hung for allegedly being witches —most of whom denied the charge.[17] The church of resident aliens had become a horde of savage warlords.

The militant, Constantinian mindset carried into the Protestant Reformation. So long as they remained a persecuted minority, Reformers generally decried the use of violence for religious purposes. But once given the power of the sword, most used it as relentlessly as it had previously been used against them. Indeed, with the exception of the Anabaptists, every splinter group of the Reformation in the sixteenth and seventeenth centuries spilled blood. Lutherans, Calvinists, Anglicans, and other Protestant groups fought each other, fought the Catholics, and martyred Anabaptists and other "heretics" by the hundreds. It wasn't until the bloodshed became economically unbearable and unfeasible in the Thirty Years' War that a truce (the Peace of Westphalia) was called and Christians agreed, at least theoretically, to end the violence.

Yet while the Christian use of the sword subsided in Europe, it continued in the New World. As God gave Canaan to Joshua, many argued, so God gave other lands over to white European Christians. To the thinking of many, the church "militant and triumphant" was on the move to conquer the world for Christ, and all who resisted it were seen as resisting God himself and deserving death.[18] Christians coming to the long-inhabited land of America participated in the slaughter of millions of Native Americans, as well as the enslavement and murder of millions of Africans as a means of conquering and establishing this new land for Jesus. Such, it was claimed, was the "manifest destiny" of Europeans,[19] and it wasn't simply warriors who died at the swords of Christians. As is common with kingdom-of-the-world conquests, raping, torturing for sport, pillaging, and treatise breaking were widespread.

While the violent expression of the Constantinian mindset has been largely outlawed, the mindset itself is very much alive today. To be sure, in some parts of the world Christians still engage in violence against other Christians, Muslims, Hindus, and other groups. But even within the borders of America, the mindset is alive and well. When Jerry Falwell, reflecting a widespread sentiment among conservative Christians, says America should hunt terrorists down and "blow them all away *in the name of the Lord*" (emphasis added), he is expressing the Constantinian mindset. When Pat Robertson declares that the United States should assassinate President Chavez of Venezuela, he also is expressing the Constantinian mindset. And when Christians try to enforce their holy will on select groups of sinners by power of law, they are essentially doing the same thing, even if the violent means of enforcing their will is no longer available to them.

A DEMONIC IRONY

It has been a profoundly sad and ironic history. In the interest of effectively accomplishing what it thought was an immediate and discernable good thing, the church often forsook its kingdom-of-God call. As a result, it frequently justified doing tremendously evil things. The moment worldly effectiveness replaces faithfulness as the motive for an individual's or institution's behavior, they are no longer acting on behalf of the kingdom of God but are participating in the kingdom of the world. The so-called good end will always be used to justify the evil means for those thinking with a kingdom-of-the-world mindset, and in doing this, the church succumbed to the very temptation Jesus resisted. It wanted to fix the world with its superior wisdom and run the world with the sword because it naively believed it could do so better than secular authorities. So, submitting itself to the cosmic "power over" god, it established itself as the ruling Caesar of the West. Far from improving on the old version of the kingdom of the world, however, it brought about a regime that was often worse than the version it replaced.

In fact, a kingdom-of-God citizen could (and should) argue that the Christian version of the kingdom of the world was actually the *worst* version the world has ever seen. For this was the version of the kingdom of the world that did the most harm to the kingdom of God. Not only did it torture and kill, as versions of the kingdom of the world frequently do—it did this under the banner of Christ. If violence and oppression are demonic, violence and oppression "in the name of Jesus" is far more so. The church of Christendom thereby brought disrepute to the name of Christ, associating his kingdom with the atrocities it carried out for centuries. The resistance most Islamic countries have to Christianity today, in fact, is partly to be explained by the vicious behavior of Christians toward Muslims throughout history.

This tragic history has to be considered one of Satan's greatest victories, and the demonic ironies abound. In the name of the one who taught us not to lord over others but rather to serve them (Matt. 20:25–28), the church often lorded over others with a vengeance as ruthless as any version of the kingdom of the world ever has. In the name of the one who taught us to turn the other cheek, the church often cut off people's heads. In the name of the one who taught us to love our enemies, the church often burned its enemies alive. In the name of the one who taught us to bless those who persecute us, the church often became a ruthless persecutor. In the name of the one who taught us to take up the cross, the church often took up the sword and nailed others to the cross. Hence, in the name of winning the world for Jesus Christ, the church often became the main obstacle to believing in Jesus Christ.

THE CHURCH VERSUS JESUS

While we, of course, have no business judging people's hearts and deciding who is and is not "saved," kingdom-of-God citizens must have a vested interest in discerning and declaring what is and is not the kingdom of God. If *we* don't declare that this barbaric religious version of the kingdom of the world was not, and is not, the kingdom of God, who will? While Christian apologists sometimes try to minimize the harm the church has done, making excuses for it whenever possible and insisting instead on the good the church accomplished, kingdom people should rather be on the front row declaring that insofar as the church picked up the sword, it had *nothing* whatsoever to do with the kingdom of God. Far from defending the church, kingdom people should lead the charge in critiquing it, for when it exercised power over others in Jesus' name, not only was it not the kingdom of God—something that is true of all versions of the kingdom of the world—it constituted a demonic distortion of the kingdom of God.

For the sake of the kingdom of God, we need to proclaim with our lives, and with our words when necessary, that the sole criteria for whether something is a manifestation of the kingdom of God or not is the person of Jesus Christ. To the extent that an individual or group looks like Jesus, dying for those who crucified him and praying for their forgiveness in the process—to that degree they can be said to manifest the kingdom of God. To the degree they do not look like this, they do not manifest God's kingdom. Hence, to the extent that the church throughout history has persecuted "sinners" and "heretics" rather than embracing them, serving them, and sacrificing for them in love, it was simply one religious version of the kingdom of the world among a multitude of others—only worse, precisely because it claimed to represent the kingdom of God.

To say the same thing a different way, kingdom people need to lead the charge in proclaiming that the church has nothing to do with the kingdom of God whenever it wields the sword instead of loving. While those who wielded the Constantinian sword throughout history undoubtedly convinced themselves they were wielding the sword in love—this is a common self-delusion among religious power brokers—lording over, torturing, and killing people does not communicate their unsurpassable worth to them; it is *not* loving.

Love is patient and kind (1 Cor. 13:4); enslaving and torturing people is neither. Love is never rude (1 Cor. 13:5); burning people alive is. Love does not insist on its own way and is not irritable or resentful when others disagree (1 Cor. 13:5); compelling people to agree with you by using force is the direct antithesis. Love doesn't rejoice in wrongdoing (1 Cor. 13:6), even if (especially if) those rejoicing credit God, who supposedly gave them the power to do it. Love bears all things while believing the best in others and hoping the best for others (1 Cor. 13:7); imprisoning, enslaving, and killing others in the name of your religious views is not bearing their burdens, believing the best about them, or hoping the best for them. It's that simple.

Given how obvious this is, one wonders how it was so often missed and why it is yet so often missed today. One wonders why no one in church history has ever been considered a heretic for being unloving. People were anathematized and often tortured and killed for disagreeing on matters of doctrine or on the authority of the church. But no one on record has ever been so much as rebuked for not loving as Christ loved.

Yet if love is to be placed above all other considerations (Col. 3:14; 1 Peter 4:8), if nothing has any value apart from love (1 Cor. 13:1–3), and if the only thing that matters is faith working in love (Gal. 5:6), how is it that possessing Christlike love has never been considered the central test of orthodoxy? How is it that those who tortured and burned heretics were not themselves considered heretics for doing so? Was this not heresy of the worst sort? How is it that those who perpetrated such things were not only not deemed heretics but often were (and yet are) held up as "heroes of the faith"?

If there is an answer to this question, I believe it lies in the deceptive power of the sword. While God uses the sword of governments to preserve law, order, and justice, as we have seen, there is a corrupting principality and power always at work. Much like the magical ring in Tolkien's *Lord of the Rings*, the sword has a demonic power to deceive us. When we pick it up, we come under its power. It convinces us that our use of violence is a justified means to a noble end. It intoxicates us with the unquenchable dream of redemptive violence and blinds us to our own iniquities, thereby making us feel righteous in overpowering the unrighteousness of others. Most of the slaughtering done throughout history has been done by people who sincerely believed they were promoting "the good." Everyone thinks *their* wars are just, if not holy. Marxists, Nazis, the Khmer Rouge, Islamic terrorists, and Christian crusaders have this in common.

KEEPING THE KINGDOM HOLY

As we have said, kingdom disciples need to be as outspoken in repudiating the dark side of church history as non-Christian critics could ever be. We should have no more interest in defending a religious version of the kingdom of the world than we have in defending an Islamic or Buddhist or Marxist version of the kingdom of the world. But we should have a great investment in criticizing it, for the Christian version hinders our call to advance the kingdom of Calvary-like love.

We need to repudiate the violent "power over" side of church history not just for the sake of others, but for our own, for we need to continually remind ourselves how easy it is to give in to the Devil's temptation and, thereby, desecrate the holiness of the kingdom. We need to always remember how subtle is the pull to be conformed "to the pattern of this world" (Rom. 12:2 NIV). We need to remain aware of how easy it is for us to be seduced by the demonic gods that pollute the American air we breath—the gods of wealth, self-centeredness, greed, racism, nationalism, and violent triumphalism. Without noticing it we can find ourselves morphing the radical gospel of Christ into a self-serving, Americanized, violent version of the kingdom of the world.

Jesus taught us that our life, prayer, and mission must be to keep the Father's name (character, reputation) holy, and to work to see his kingdom come "on earth as it is in heaven" (Matt. 6:9–10). To the extent that we fail to do this, we fail to obey Christ's commission and example. Yet as history testifies, nothing is easier for us than to give in to the Devil's temptation to do just this. Indeed, all indications are that we American Christians have, to a large degree, already succumbed to this very temptation and have been doing so throughout our nation's history.

The kingdom of God is not a Christian version of the kingdom of the world. It is, rather, a holy alternative to all versions of the kingdom of the world, and everything hangs on kingdom people appreciating this uniqueness and preserving this holiness. We must always remember that we are "resident aliens" in this oppressed world, soldiers of the kingdom of God stationed behind enemy lines with a unique, all consuming, holy calling on our life. We are called, individually and corporately, to look like Jesus to a rebellious, self-centered, and violent world.

CHAPTER 5

TAKING AMERICA BACK FOR GOD

But Jesus called them to him and said, "You know that the rulers of the Gentiles lord it over them, and their great ones are tyrants over them. It will not be so among you; but whoever wishes to be great among you must be your servant, and whoever wishes to be first among you must be your slave; just as the Son of Man came not to be served but to serve, and to give his life a ransom for many."

MATTHEW 20:25–28

Every war ... with all its ordinary consequences ... the murder with the justifications of its necessity and justice, the exaltation and glorification of military exploits, the worship of the flag, the patriotic sentiments ... and so on, does more in one year to pervert men's minds than thousands of robberies, murders, and arsons perpetrated during hundreds of years by individual men under the influence of passion.

LEO TOLSTOY[1]

Having accepted the falsehood that we must run the world, we seek to get hold of the mantle of power. Consequently, "discipleship" gets transformed: "following Jesus," rather than denoting a walking in the way of the humble Suffering Servant, denotes being "spiritual" as we seek to wield power over our fellows.... Christians become convinced that they are pursuing the purposes of God by pursuing the purposes of the empire.

LEE CAMP[2]

AN IDOLATROUS CELEBRATION

Shortly after the Gulf War in 1992 I happened to visit a July Fourth worship service at a certain megachurch. At center stage in this auditorium stood a large cross next to an equally large American flag. The congregation sang some praise choruses mixed with such patriotic hymns as "God Bless America." The climax of the service centered on a video of a well-known Christian military general giving a patriotic speech about how God has blessed America and blessed its military troops, as evidenced by the speedy and almost "casualty-free" victory "he gave us" in the Gulf War (Iraqi deaths apparently weren't counted as "casualties" worthy of notice). Triumphant military music played in the background as he spoke.

The video closed with a scene of a silhouette of three crosses on a hill with an American flag waving in the background. Majestic, patriotic music now thundered. Suddenly, four fighter jets appeared on the horizon, flew over the crosses, and then split apart. As they roared over the camera, the words "God Bless America" appeared on the screen in front of the crosses.

The congregation responded with roaring applause, catcalls, and a standing ovation. I saw several people wiping tears from their eyes. Indeed, as I remained frozen in my seat, I grew teary-eyed as well—but for entirely different reasons. I was struck with horrified grief.

Thoughts raced through my mind: How could the cross and the sword have been so thoroughly fused without anyone seeming to notice? How could Jesus' self-sacrificial death be linked with flying killing machines? How could Calvary be associated with bombs and missiles? How could Jesus' people applaud tragic violence, regardless of why it happened and regardless of how they might benefit from its outcome? How could the kingdom of God be reduced to this sort of violent, nationalistic tribalism? Has the church progressed at all since the Crusades?

Indeed, I wondered how this tribalistic, militaristic, religious celebration was any different from the one I had recently witnessed on television carried out by Taliban Muslims raising their guns as they joyfully praised Allah for the victories they believed "he had given them" in Afghanistan?

Now, perhaps one could respond to my many questions by insisting that the Gulf War, unlike the war carried out by the Taliban, was a "just war." After all, the Kuwaiti people were losing their freedom and there were reports of women being raped.

Perhaps it was; perhaps it wasn't. People still debate this.[3] But as kingdom-of-God citizens who are to always have a healthy suspicion toward every version of the kingdom of the world, especially our own, we have to at least ask the question why the loss of freedom to the Kuwaiti people mattered so much to our government while the loss of freedom to millions of others around the globe does not? For example, less than two years after the Gulf War, nearly a million Rwandans were barbarically massacred in a three-month period. Though the American government and other Western governments possessed detailed information about the genocide as it was unfolding, we did nothing. A similar question could be raised, comparing our war for "Iraqi freedom" with our reluctance to get involved militarily in the Sudan, where atrocities—far worse and on a larger scale than those perpetrated by Saddam Hussein—have been carried out routinely.

Of course, the reasons why we go to war in Kuwait and Iraq but do little to help Rwanda or the Sudan are complex. Kingdom-of-the-world issues almost always are, especially when they pertain to international relations. But for kingdom-of-God citizens who are aware of the idolatrous self-centeredness of rebellious hearts and the universal influence of Satan, and who thus know better than to place undue trust in any version of the kingdom of the world, don't these inconsistencies at least call into question the claim that we as a nation operate with purely altruistic motives? Don't these inconsistencies suggest that *where* a group is located and *what* their resources are (like oil) are at least one factor in whether a people's freedom is worth risking American lives for? In other words, doesn't it suggest that, like every other version of the kingdom of the world, America looks out primarily for its own self-interest? And shouldn't this curb our confidence that God is always on our side and shares our excitement over "winning"?[4]

My goal in raising these questions is not to critique America. To the contrary, this is the way *all* versions of the kingdom of the world operate. My critique is rather toward *the American church*. We expect nations to be driven by self-interest, but we shouldn't expect kingdom people to applaud this fact, especially when the national self-interest involves taking lives! Isn't our central calling as kingdom people to manifest the truth that this old, self-centered, tribalistic, violent way of living has been done away in Christ? Are we not to display the truth that in Christ a new humanity has been created, one in which there are no ethnic, nationalistic, gender, social, or economic distinctions (Eph. 2:13–17; Gal. 3:26–29)? Aren't we called to "live by the Spirit" and thus put away all "works of the flesh"—including aligning ourselves with various sides of "dissensions [and] factions" (Gal. 5:16–20)?

Whether one thinks the Gulf War was just or not (or whether one thinks this question is even relevant for disciples of Jesus), how can kingdom people not grieve the loss of Iraqi lives as much as the loss of American lives? Didn't Jesus die for Iraqis as much as for Americans? Don't they possess the same unsurpassable worth that Americans possess? Are we not to embody and manifest Christ's Calvary-quality love even for our nation's worst enemies? When a congregation, gathered in the name of the crucified Nazarene, applauds the violent conquest of fighter jets flying over his cross, is this not further evidence of the diabolic power of the sword to blind us?

THE ALL-TOO-COMMON RALLY CRY

While I suspect—and hope—the fusion of patriotism with the kingdom of God I witnessed in that July Fourth video is not representative of most conservative churches, I also know that the basic sentiment it expressed *is* far too typical. The evangelical church in America has, to a large extent, been co-opted by an American, religious version of the kingdom of the world. We have come to trust the power of the sword more than the power of the cross. We have become intoxicated with the Constantinian, nationalistic, violent mindset of imperialistic Christendom.[5]

The evidence of this is all around but nowhere clearer than in the simple, oft-repeated, slogan that we Christians are going to "take America back for God." The thinking is that America was founded as a Christian nation but has simply veered off track.[6] If we can just get the power of Caesar again, however, we can take it back. If we can just get more Christians into office, pass more Christian laws, support more Christian policies, we can restore this nation to its "one nation under God" status. If we can just protect the sanctity of marriage, make it difficult, if not impossible, to live a gay lifestyle, and overturn Roe vs. Wade, we will be getting closer. If we can just get prayer (Christian prayer, of course) back into our schools along with the Ten Commandments and creationist teaching, we will be restoring our country's Christian heritage. If we can just keep "one nation under God" in our Pledge of Allegiance, protect the rights of Christians to speak their minds, get more control of the liberal media, clean up the trash that's coming out of the movie and record industry, while marginalizing, if not eradicating, liberal groups such as the ACLU, we will have won this nation back for Jesus Christ.

Yes, the thinking goes, if only we can get Christian people and Christian ideas to dominate the political landscape, we will have won the culture war and God will be glorified. It will be good for God and good for all Americans (indeed, for the world). For we, being the true people of God, know God's will better than others and, thus, know better than pagans what is good for a nation. Few things can get a typical conservative Christian gathering as fired up as a message that hammers on topics such as these.

The position is exceedingly popular, but as people whose ultimate allegiance is to the kingdom of God and not to any version of the kingdom of the world, we have to ask ourselves several very sobering questions.

THE LACK OF PRECEDENT

First, since we are called to mimic Jesus in all we do as citizens of the kingdom of God, we have to ask: When did Jesus ever act or talk like this? If ever there was an instance where the kingdom of

God and worldly politics could justifiably have been fused, and if ever there was an instance where one could justifiably have argued for "taking a nation back for God," it was first-century Israel. Unlike America, Israel *was*, in fact, called to be a "nation under God" in a unique way. God was supposed to be her king and, moreover, most of Jesus' Jewish contemporaries wanted to "take Israel back for God." This is precisely why they continually tried to fit Jesus into the mold of a political messiah.

Yet Jesus consistently declined, thereby showing that God's mode of operation in the world was no longer going to be nationalistic. As Trocme notes, "There is a complete break between the old Israel, ending at the cross, and the new Israel, the church, that grows out of the resurrection and the coming of the Spirit at Pentecost."[7] While God had intended to use Israel to reach the world (among other things), this was going to be his approach no longer. Instead, beginning with Christ, God was going to redeem the world through a "mustard-seed" kingdom comprised of people from every tribe and nation. The kingdom Jesus came to establish would be one that found absolutely no significance in nationalistic allegiances, so no longer would there be "Jew or Greek" (Gal. 3:28). If Jesus wasn't concerned about "taking Israel back for God" by political means, why would any who align themselves with his kingdom aspire to "take America back for God" by these means?

The point I'm making can be broadened beyond Jesus' stance toward Israel. Consider these questions: Did Jesus ever suggest by word or by example that we should aspire to acquire, let alone take over, the power of Caesar? Did Jesus spend any time and energy trying to improve, let alone dominate, the reigning government of his day? Did he ever work to pass laws against the sinners he hung out with and ministered to? Did he worry at all about ensuring that his rights and the religious rights of his followers were protected? Does *any* author in the New Testament remotely hint that engaging in this sort of activity has anything to do with the kingdom of God?

The answer to all these questions is, of course, *no*. And since Jesus is our example and the New Testament our constitution, does this not tell us that however we, as American citizens, might personally decide to weigh in on these issues politically, we should not attach the label *Christian* to this activity? You may or may not think it good for the country to outlaw gay marriage or keep the phrase "under God" in the Pledge of Allegiance, for example; but isn't the lack of precedent in Jesus' ministry or the rest of the New Testament enough to demonstrate that your views on these matters, as right (or wrong) as they may be, are not part of your distinctive kingdom-of-God calling?

Of course our political views will be influenced by our Christian faith. We may even believe that our views, if they are implemented, will help facilitate the advancement of the kingdom. But we must also recognize that people who have diametrically opposing views may believe *they too* are advancing the kingdom, which is all well and good so long as we don't christen our views as *the* Christian view. As people whose citizenship is in heaven before it is in any nation (Phil. 3:20), and whose kingdom identity is rooted in Jesus rather than in a political agenda, we must never forget that the only way we individually and collectively represent the kingdom of God is through loving, Christlike, sacrificial acts of service to others. Anything and everything else, however good and noble, lies outside the kingdom of God.

A PLAUSIBLE TEMPTATION

Some will insist that the only reason that neither Jesus nor anyone else in the first several centuries of the church tried to dominate the political system of their day was because they were simply unable to do so. After all, the earliest Christians were a small minority of people living in a nondemocratic and hostile environment. By contrast, the argument goes, American Christians are a sizable group living in a rather friendly, democratic (if not Christian) land, and we *are* able to at least vastly improve, if not someday dominate, our government and culture. And since to whom much is given much is required (Luke 12:48), do we not have a spiritual and moral obligation to use this opportunity to the full advantage of the kingdom of God? In this light, the argument concludes, to shirk the opportunity to rule because we are afraid of compromising our kingdom calling is irresponsible, pharisaical, and cowardly. The argument seems to make so much sense—and therein lies the temptation.

Recall that the Constantinian church explained away the self-sacrificial love and humility of Jesus and the early church in just this fashion. Instead of constituting the essence of the kingdom of God, the self-sacrificial and humble example of Jesus and the early church was understood to be merely a provisional inconvenience. Now that God had supposedly given the church power to rule, they reasoned, it just made sense to use it. For they, being the people who knew the truth, obviously knew best how to rule others.

Yet what did this line of reasoning accomplish? It produced centuries of barbaric bloodshed—in Jesus' name. Beyond the tragedy of millions of people being brutally murdered, the fact that this was done under the banner of the cross has harmed global missions for centuries. What is more, wherever this line of reasoning was carried out, it inevitably damaged the church.

Can you find any region where Christians once ruled where the church has prospered over the long run? Scan the whole of Europe: England, Sweden, Denmark, and so on. Could anyone dispute that these countries are today on the whole *more* secular and *less* open to the gospel than regions that have had little or no contact with the gospel? And while there are pockets of vibrant kingdom gatherings in these countries, don't the mostly empty, large church buildings in these countries testify to the long-term damaging effect that Christian rule has had on the church?

What does this tell us? It teaches us that whenever Christians have gotten what so many American evangelicals today are trying to get—namely, the power to enforce their righteous will on others—it eventually harms the church as well as the culture. The lesson of history, a lesson the Devil has known all along, is this: The best way to defeat the kingdom of God is to empower the church to rule the kingdom of the world—for then it *becomes* the kingdom of the world! The best way to get people to lay down the cross is to hand them the sword!

While this conclusion may seem paradoxical to the Constantinian kingdom-of-the-world mindset, it makes perfect sense within a kingdom-of-God mindset. For the kingdom of God is not about coercive "power over," but influential "power under." Its essence is found in the power to transform lives from the inside out through love and service.

When kingdom-of-God citizens aspire to acquire Caesar's authority to accomplish "the good," we sell our kingdom birthright for a bowl of worldly porridge (Gen. 25:29–34). To the extent that we pick up the sword, we put down the cross. When our goal as kingdom people becomes centered on effectively running a better (let alone Christian) version of the kingdom of the world, we compromise our calling to be faithful to the kingdom of God.

John Howard Yoder eloquently makes the point when he writes:

> The vision of ultimate good being determined by faithfulness and not by results is the point where we moderns get off. We confuse the kind of "triumph of the good," whose sole guarantee is the resurrection and the premise of the eternal glory of the Lamb, with an immediately accessible triumph which can be manipulated, just past the next social action campaign, by getting hold of society as a whole at the top. What in the Middle Ages was done by Roman Christianity or Islam is now being attempted by Marxism and by democratic nationalism....
>
> We may well prefer a democratically controlled oligarchy to some other kind. We may well have a choice between Marxist and Islamic and other statements of the vision of the good society. But what our contemporaries find themselves practically incapable of challenging is that the social problem can be solved by determining which aristocrats are morally justified, by virtue of their better ideology, to use the power

of society from the top so as to lead the whole system in their direction.[8]

The unchallenged assumption is that society's problems can be solved by getting the right version of the kingdom of the world—the right aristocrats—in power at the top of the society, and that if only the right people acquire the power to lead society in the right direction, then all will be well. This "power over" kingdom-of-the-world assumption has dominated much Christian and Islamic thought throughout history, with catastrophic consequences, and it obviously continues to influence the thinking of many Christians and non-Christians today. If only Matthew's conservative program or Simon's radical program can win, then we will fix the world and God will be glorified.

It is understandable that secularists would accept this assumption, for they can conceive of no other solution to society's problems, but kingdom-of-God citizens are empowered to have keener vision. Indeed, the assumption that society's problems can be solved by empowering the right ideology, whether this be a democratic, Marxist, Islamic, or Christian ideology, constitutes a fundamental denial of the lordship of Christ. As such, it constitutes a rejection of the reality of the kingdom of God and the distinctive call of the disciple of Christ to manifest this reality.

This kingdom-of-the-world assumption—to conquer the world for the glory of God—is in essence the very thing the Devil tempted Jesus with. What makes the assumption so tempting is that it makes so much sense. How could society fail to be better off if we who know the truth are empowered to get our way in society?

The point is so obvious, it seems, that we might be inclined to accept Christendom's traditional rationalization that the only reason Jesus and the early church didn't try to gain power over others was because they couldn't. Yet as plausible as this way of thinking may be from within the world's "power over" paradigm, it is utterly absurd when we view it from within God's "power under" paradigm.

Think about it. The Son of God couldn't exercise "power over"?! He certainly could have, for this is precisely what the Devil offered him! Even apart from this, Jesus had legions of angels at his beck and call and the power of God Almighty at his disposal. Had he wanted to, Jesus could easily have become a victorious Caesar rather than a crucified Savior.

Jesus refused to call on these angels not because he and his disciples hadn't yet acquired enough power from Caesar, such as Augustine had in the fourth and fifth centuries, but because doing so would have violated the heart of the kingdom he came to establish. To reveal the holiness of God's kingdom, Jesus voluntarily "emptied himself," "humbled himself," and took on the form of a servant, allowing himself to be crucified for the sake of others and for the glory of God (Phil. 2:6–8). In doing so, writes Yoder, "Christ renounced the claim to govern history," choosing instead to win the world through sacrificial, loving submission.[9]

This is the heart of God's kingdom, and this is the mind of Christ that all who claim to follow Christ are commanded to have (Phil. 2:5). Thus, to the disciple of Christ, the power of the sword must be forever viewed as a demonic temptation, not a viable, let alone Christian, solution.

The age-old temptation to seize "power over" is exacerbated for American Christians by virtue of the fact that our government invites us to participate in running our version of the kingdom of the world. Christians living in communist or totalitarian regimes don't have this option or this temptation. In my opinion, the ability to participate in the running of a country is a wonderful kingdom-of-the-world privilege —arguably the best privilege any version of the kingdom of the world can give its subjects. But as valuable as it is, kingdom-of-God citizens must consistently resist the temptation to identify our ability to influence government by voting or serving in a governmental office as our distinct authority as kingdom people. We are kingdom people who happen to live in a context where we may exercise some authority, but the governmental authority we may exercise is not our distinct authority as kingdom people.

To be clear, a kingdom person may be called by God to serve in a certain governmental capacity, and in this sense their individual calling may be manifested in how they carry out their office. But their unique authority as a kingdom person cannot be equated with their governmental authority, just as it cannot be equated with our ability to vote. Rather, our unique kingdom-of-God authority resides exclusively in our ability and willingness to come under people in sacrificial love, a unique authority that cannot be given by Caesar and cannot be taken by Caesar.[10]

Our unique kingdom authority and calling is given by God, and it looks the same whether we are a governor or a plumber, whether we live in America, North Korea, Iran, or Sweden. It may take a million different forms, but it always looks like Jesus Christ, dying in love for the people who crucified him.

TAKING "BACK" AMERICA FOR GOD?

The first question we needed to address in response to the popular "Take America Back for God" slogan concerned the precedent of Jesus, and in this light we must judge that the slogan can lead us into temptation. The second concerns the meaning of the slogan itself. I, for one, confess to being utterly mystified by the phrase. If we are to take America *back* for God, it must have once belonged to God, but it's not at all clear when this golden Christian age was.

Were these God-glorifying years before, during, or after Europeans "discovered" America and carried out the doctrine of "manifest destiny"—the belief that God (or, for some, nature) had destined white Christians to conquer the native inhabitants and steal their land? Were the God-glorifying years the ones in which whites massacred these natives by the millions, broke just about every covenant they ever made with them, and then forced survivors onto isolated reservations? Was the golden age before, during, or after white Christians loaded five to six million Africans on cargo ships to bring them to their newfound country, enslaving the three million or so who actually survived the brutal trip? Was it during the two centuries when Americans acquired remarkable wealth by the sweat and blood of their slaves? Was this the time when we were truly "one nation under God," the blessed time that so many evangelicals seem to want to take our nation *back* to?[11]

Maybe someone would suggest that the golden age occurred after the Civil War, when blacks were finally freed. That doesn't quite work either, however, for the virtual apartheid that followed under Jim Crow laws—along with the ongoing violence, injustices, and dishonesty toward Native Americans and other nonwhites up into the early twentieth century—was hardly "God-glorifying." (In this light, it should come as no surprise to find that few Christian Native Americans, African-Americans, or other nonwhites join in the chorus that we need to "Take America Back for God.")

If we look at historical reality rather than pious verbiage, it's obvious that America never really "belonged to God."[12] As we've said, when the kingdom of God is manifested, it's obvious. It looks like Jesus. But America as a nation has clearly never looked remotely like Jesus. There was nothing distinctively Christlike about the way America was "discovered," conquered, or governed in the early years. To the contrary, the way this nation was "discovered," conquered, and governed was a rather typical, barbaric, violent, kingdom-of-the-world affair. The immoral barbarism displayed in the early (and subsequent) years of this country was, sadly, pretty typical by kingdom-of-the-world standards. The fact that it was largely done under the banner of Christ doesn't make it more Christian, any more than any other bloody conquest done in Jesus' name throughout history (such as the Crusades and the Inquisition) qualifies them as Christlike.

In fact, we should view the fact that Europeans conquered under the banner of Christ to be just another typical kingdom-of-the-world behavior. As noted in chapter 1, kingdom-of-the-world armies have usually fought under the banner of their nationalist religion and invoked their tribal deities as they fought. Indeed, most kingdom-of-the-world warriors have believed they were killing or dying for a "manifest destiny." They believed God, or particular gods, were on their side and would give them victory. Most conquests have had a religious dimension, if only because it's hard to motivate one group to kill another and be willing to be killed by others without convincing them that there's a religious dimension to their tribal cause.

The European conquering of America was simply another all-too-typical version of this kingdom-of-the-world behavior. From the kingdom-of-God perspective, the fact that Christ happened to be the national warrior deity invoked to carry out whites' "manifest destiny"—inspiring them to kill, cheat, marginalize, and enslave native Americans and Africans (as well as other nonwhite groups)—simply means that this particular kingdom-of-the-world episode was more damaging to the cause of the kingdom of God than others.

This, of course, is not what most American Christians (especially most *white* Americans) who love their country want to hear. I completely understand this. Yet if we simply stick to the truth that only what looks like Jesus qualifies as kingdom-of-God activity, there is no way to avoid this conclusion. Slaughtering, enslaving, cheating, conquering, and dominating are not the sort of activities Jesus engaged in!

ONE NATION UNDER GOD

Those who want to enlist the power of Caesar to "take America back for God" usually appeal to the alleged fact that the founding fathers were stalwart Christians who established America as "one nation under God." The notion is that the founders intended America to be a Christian nation, established on Christian laws and exemplifying Christian morality. *This* is what many want to take America back to.

There has been a great deal of debate about the extent to which the founding fathers were Christian in any historic orthodox sense of the term. My own research inclines me to conclude that most were more deistic than Christian, and that they collectively had no intention of founding an explicitly Christian nation.[13] At the very least, it's significant that the Declaration of Independence proclaims truths that the founding fathers thought to be "self-evident" to *natural reason* (a very deistic idea), not truths that are *scriptural*. Also, our country's Constitution is based on reason, not the Bible. It is, in my estimation, a truly amazing document, yet it owes more to John Locke than it does to the Bible.

But the issue of what various founding fathers personally believed is really irrelevant to the issue at hand. For even if they believed they were in some sense establishing a Christian nation, as some maintain, it remains perfectly clear that it never has actually looked like Christ. We have only to listen to the voices of nonwhites throughout our history to appreciate this fact.

Just listen to Frederick Douglass, a nineteenth-century slave who taught himself how to read and write, as he expresses his view of how Christian America was:

> Between the Christianity of this land, and the Christianity of Christ, I recognize the widest possible difference—so wide, that to receive the one as good, pure, and holy, is of necessity to reject the other as bad, corrupt and wicked.... I love the pure, peaceable, and impartial Christianity of Christ; I therefore hate the corrupt, slaveholding, women-whipping, cradle-plundering, partial and hypocritical Christianity of this land. Indeed, I can see no reason, but the most deceitful one, for calling the religion of this land Christianity.[14]

When we suggest that this nation was once Christian, we participate in the racist and demonic deceit that Douglass poignantly exposes. To avoid this deceit, it is also helpful to remember that most of the violence and dishonesty carried out against the native Americans occurred *after* America was founded as a nation "under God." Likewise, the Supreme Court's decision that blacks were only three-fifths human came long after America was purportedly established as a Christian nation. The list of ways that early America didn't look remotely look like the domain in which God is king—indeed, the ways America has often looked the opposite—could be expanded indefinitely.

But even the un-Christlike behavior of America as a nation is not the most fundamental issue. The foundational issue is whether *any* "power over" kingdom could ever be Christian—even if it wanted to. We have argued that being Christlike is not, and cannot be, an ideal to which any version of the kingdom of the world can aspire, let alone claim for itself. As much as God wants governments to operate justly, Jesus didn't come to establish a perfect worldly government. He came to establish the kingdom of God as a radical alternative to all versions of the kingdom of the world, whether they declare themselves to be "under God" or not.

When we misguidedly loop Christian talk into American kingdom-of-the-world talk, we do great harm to the work of the kingdom of God. Among other things, we leverage the credibility of God's kingdom on someone believing that it was God's will—"manifest destiny"—for whites to carry out the barbarism they carried out toward Native Americans, Africans, and a host of other nonwhites in the course of American history. We compromise the purity and beauty—the *holiness*—of the kingdom of God by associating it with the typical "power over" injustices that this country has largely been built on. And we encourage the sort of "power over" behavior among religious people that we see today as they attempt to "take America back for God" by political means. Allegiance to the kingdom of God is confused with allegiance to America, and lives that are called to be spent serving others are spent trying to gain power over others.

THE GOOD AND THE BEAUTIFUL

When we clearly and consistently separate the kingdom of God from all versions of the kingdom of the world, we are in a position to affirm the good as well as the bad of American history without having to defend it as Christian. For example, insofar as one could argue that it served justice, one could argue it was better that America won independence from England, despite the massive bloodshed the fight for independence required. But neither the outcome nor the bloody process that led to it were Christlike. It didn't manifest the kingdom of God, for Jesus never killed people to acquire political freedom for himself or others. Hence, July Fourth is not—or at least should not be—a Christian holiday, however meaningful it may be to some Americans.

Still, a citizen of the kingdom of God need not deny the positive outcomes that have resulted from Europeans discovering and conquering America. Yes, the process was largely immoral and extremely bloody, as it typically is when versions of the kingdom of the world collide. But the bloody injustices don't negate the fact that America has arguably now become, by historic and global standards, a relatively good version of the kingdom of the world. Still, we must never confuse the positive things that America does with the kingdom of God, for the kingdom of God is not centered on being morally, politically, or socially positive *relative* to other versions of the kingdom of the world. Rather, the kingdom of God is centered on being *beautiful*, as defined by Jesus Christ dying on a cross for those who crucified him.

To promote law, order, and justice is good, and we certainly should do all we can to support this. But to love enemies, forgive transgressors, bless persecutors, serve sinners, accept social rejects, abolish racist walls, share resources with the poor, bear the burden of neighbors, suffer with the oppressed—all the while making no claims to promote oneself—*this* is beautiful; *this* is Christlike. Only this, therefore, is distinct kingdom-of-God activity.

WINNING BACK THE WORLD

I should end this chapter by saying that, as misleading and dangerous as the slogan "Take America Back for God" is, there is a profound element of truth in it. For as citizens of the kingdom of God, we *are* called to win back America for Jesus Christ—as well as Europe, Iraq, Sudan, Rwanda, and the rest of the world. But everything hangs upon *how* we believe we are to do this. What power do we trust?

If we think for a moment that we are fulfilling the commission to take the world back for God by acquiring the ability to control behavior through the power of the sword, we are deceived. If we suppose that America, Europe, or any nation is closer to the kingdom of God because certain Christian ideals dominate the political landscape, it is evidence that we have bought into the temptation to trust the sword rather than the cross. If we think we can tweak any version of the kingdom of the world to make it into the kingdom of God, we thereby reveal that our thinking has been co-opted by the kingdom of the world. Again, the only way the world can be won for Jesus Christ is by people being transformed from the inside out through the power of Christ's love expressed through the Calvary-quality service of his followers.

The question that wins the world is not, how can we get our "morally superior" way enforced in the world? The question that wins the world, and the question that must define the individual and collective life of kingdom-of-God citizens is, how do we take up the cross for the world? How do we best communicate to others their unsurpassable worth before God? How do we serve and wash the feet of the oppressed and despised?

We conquer not by the power of the sword but "by the blood of the Lamb and by the word of [our] testimony." We conquer by not clinging "to life even in the face of death" (Rev. 12:11); we conquer by refusing to place our trust in the violent "power over" kingdom of the world, while instead making it our sole task, moment by moment, to manifest the unique righteousness of the kingdom of God (Matt. 6:33). God in principle won the world through the Lamb's loving sacrifice, and he's in the process of manifesting this victory throughout the world through us as we replicate the Lamb's loving sacrifice in our lives. This is the kingdom of God; this is how the kingdom of God advances. And this is how the kingdom of the world will ultimately become the kingdom of the Lamb (Rev. 11:15).

If your response is that this "power under" approach is impractical, if not morally irresponsible, perhaps this too reveals that you have been conformed to the pattern of the world (Rom. 12:2) and have allowed yourself to trust "power over" rather than "power under." Perhaps it reveals that you have placed more faith in worldly "common sense" than in the resurrection. Perhaps it reveals that worldly effectiveness has replaced kingdom faithfulness as your primary concern.

When Jesus was crucified, it *looked* as if he were losing. More often than not, when the kingdom of God is being authentically carried out, it looks that way, at least initially. The cross didn't look effective on Good Friday, but God raised up Jesus on the third day. And our task is to believe that, however much it looks like we may be losing, God will use our Calvary-quality acts of service to redeem the world and build his kingdom. However much we lose—even if it's our own life—we are to believe in the resurrection. Ultimately God wins, and each one of our acts of loving self-denial will eventually be shown to have played a role in this victory.

This is faith in the resurrection. This is the kingdom of God.

CHAPTER 6

THE MYTH OF A
CHRISTIAN NATION

The words and acts of the founding fathers,
especially the first few presidents, shaped the form and
tone of the civil religion as it has been maintained ever since.
Though much is selectively derived from Christianity,
this religion is clearly not itself Christianity.

ROBERT BELLAH[1]

AS WE HAVE NOTED, MANY CHRISTIANS BELIEVE THAT AMERICA IS, OR AT
least once was, a Christian nation. We have argued that this notion
is inaccurate for the simple reason that *Christian* means "Christlike," and there never was a time when America as a nation has
acted Christlike. Indeed, we have argued that it's impossible for
any version of the kingdom of the world to be Christlike for the
simple reason that they participate in a system of domination that
necessarily places its trust in the power of the sword. It may use this
power in just or unjust ways—and we should certainly do all we
can do to influence the former and resist the latter—but in neither
case can it be said to be acting like Christ. The kingdom of God,
which always looks like Jesus, is not simply an improved version of
the kingdom of the world, for a version of the kingdom of the world
may be relatively good, but it cannot be beautiful.

In my opinion, nothing has been more damaging to the advancement of the beautiful kingdom in America, and to a significant
degree around the globe, than this myth that America is a Christian nation. In this and the following two chapters I shall discuss
five negative consequences that have resulted from this myth.

FOR GOD AND COUNTRY

First, the myth of a Christian nation harms global missions, and a little background will help explain this.

Since the time of Constantine, Christianity has largely been the obedient servant of the kingdom of the world, while the cross has often been reduced to the pole upon which a national flag waves. When leaders of so-called Christian nations felt the need to go to war to protect or expand the interests of their nation, they could often count on the church to call on God to bless its violent campaign and use its authority to motivate warriors to fight for their cause "in Jesus' name." However much leaders were driven by power or economic concerns, their cause could be made "holy" by convincing Christian subjects that God was involved. Hence, when any group had to be vanquished in the interest of the Christian nation, it has often been carried out under the banner of Christ—even when the enemy was other professing Christians. "For God and country" has been the battle cry of Christians, as it has in one form or another for almost every other army, whatever the particular religion or nation.

When America was founded as a British colony, this traditional Constantinian "God and country" sentiment reigned, and when America broke from England, it continued to reign. Though America is now largely secularized, this Constantinian perspective continues to reign, though in a more secularized, subdued form. Many still believe we fight "for God and country," and leaders continue to use this faith to their full advantage whenever possible.

AMERICA AS THE LIGHT OF THE WORLD

A stunningly clear example of this was (and as of this writing, still is) the heavy use of religious rhetoric to support the invasion of Iraq and the ongoing fight against terrorism. Instead of simply arguing that it was in America's national interest to go to war—a claim that some would accept and others reject—many religious leaders and some politicians invoked God's name in support of this cause, just as the extremist Muslims did. As in the medieval Crusades, "Abba" has once again been pitted against "Allah." Many even argued that supporting the war against the Taliban and Saddam Hussein was a "Christian duty."

This Christianization of military force was strongly reinforced when President George W. Bush depicted America as being on a holy "crusade" against "evildoers." Elsewhere he said that America is the "light of the world," which the "darkness" (that is, our national enemies) could not extinguish.[2] He was of course quoting Scripture in making his point—Scripture that refers to Jesus (John 1:1–5). The fact that evangelicals as a whole were not shocked by this idolatrous association is, in my opinion, evidence of how thoroughly we have accepted the Americanized, Constantinian paradigm. In this paradigm, what applies to Jesus ("the light of the world") can be applied to our country, and what applies to Satan ("the darkness") can be applied to whomever resists our country. *We* are of God; *they* are of the Devil. *We* are the light; *they* are the darkness. Our wars are therefore "holy" wars.[3] With all due respect, this is blatant idolatry.

That a political leader would use religious rhetoric to rally people around a military cause is not surprising. This is typical in all versions of the kingdom of the world. What is surprising, and cause for great concern, is that many evangelicals were not only *not* disturbed by this—they *applauded* it.

THE HARM TO GLOBAL MISSIONS

While history proves that it's usually in a nation's self-interest to use religion and religious rhetoric to advance its causes, kingdom-of-God citizens need to see how harmful it is to the advancement of the kingdom of God. Among other things, when we associate Jesus with America, even in the most remote ways, we legitimize the widespread global perception that the Christian faith can be judged on the basis of what America has done in the past or continues to do in the present.

Now, this isn't all bad. America has done and continues to do good things around the world, for which we should be thankful. But it's also done some bad things—or at least things perceived by some to be bad. Though many Americans, including President George W. Bush, seem unable to appreciate it, there are reasons why a significant percentage of people around the globe despise us.[4] Not only does America represent greed, violence, and sexual immorality to them, but they view America as exploitive and opportunistic. To their way of thinking, for example, the 2002 invasion of Iraq, largely in defiance of the United Nations, on the later disproven grounds that Saddam Hussein posed an "imminent threat" because he was building "weapons of mass destruction," simply confirms a long history of U.S. aggression under the guise of "spreading freedom." When President Bush repeatedly says that America has a responsibility to spread freedom throughout the world, what some people around the globe hear is that American imperialism is alive and well and that we are planning on aggressively bringing other governments under our control for self-serving purposes.

Now, whether this perception is justified or not is not my immediate concern. What is a concern—and should be the primary concern for all kingdom-of-God people—is that this disdain gets associated with Christ when America is identified as a Christian nation. The tragic irony is that those who should be most vehemently denying the association for the purpose of preserving the beautiful holiness of the kingdom of God—in contrast to what America represents to many people—are the primary ones insisting on the identification! The result is that it has become humanly impossible for many around the globe to hear the good news as *good*. Instead, because of its kingdom-of-the-world associations, they hear the gospel as *bad* news, as *American* news, *exploitive capitalistic* news, *greedy* news, *violent* news, and *morally decadent* news. They can't see the beauty of the cross because everything the American flag represents to them is in the way.

As a result, global missions have been tremendously harmed by American nationalism. And we who seek first the kingdom of God

(Matt. 6:33) must accept responsibility for this. We have not placed the preservation of the holiness—the radical distinctness—of the kingdom of God as our top priority. We have rather allowed the cross to become associated with the sword of Constantine. We have allowed the unblemished beauty of Calvary to get wrapped up in the typical ugliness of our version of the kingdom of the world. We have allowed our allegiance to the kingdom of God to be compromised by allegiance to our nation. We have far too often placed our worldly citizenship before our heavenly citizenship (Phil. 3:20) and allowed the flag to smother the cross.

The time to turn completely from this Constantinian idolatry is long overdue. For God's sake—literally—we who profess allegiance to Jesus Christ must commit ourselves to proclaiming in action and word the truth that the kingdom of God *always* looks like him. Since our ultimate allegiance is not to our nation or institution, we should be on the front lines proclaiming that the history and activity of our nation has nothing to do with the kingdom of God. Far from invoking God's name to justify the behavior of our nation (for example, to "blow [people] away in the name of the Lord"), we should in God's name lead the charge in prophetically critiquing our nation. Indeed, following the example of Jesus (which is, after all, our sole calling), we should publicly side with all who have been or continue to be harmed by our nation.

CIVIL RELIGION AND THE KINGDOM OF GOD

Not only are foreign missions harmed by the pervasive myth of a Christian nation, missionary work inside our own country has been harmed, for this foundational myth reinforces the pervasive misconception that the civil religion of Christianity in America is *real* Christianity.

To understand this, we need to understand that throughout history most cultures have been influenced by some religion or other. Typically, most people in the culture don't make the dominant religion the central point of their life. But the religion nevertheless plays an important role in providing the culture with a shared worldview, shared history, shared values and practices, common holidays, and so on. In short, it helps bind the culture together. We might think of this as the civil role of religion.[5]

While legitimate debate continues about what various founding fathers of America actually believed, it is undeniable that the civil religion of America from the start has been a deistic version of Christianity. Our worldview, our sense of history, our values, and even our calendar have been influenced far more by Christianity than any other religion. While things are changing quickly, a majority of Americans still identify themselves as "Christian" to pollsters.

Now, as is typical of civil religions, if one further inquires into what actual impact these people's faith has on their lives, one discovers that in the majority of cases it is negligible. Indeed, research has consistently demonstrated that the majority of professing Christians, when asked, lack even an elementary understanding of the faith they profess.[6] Though they may attend church on occasion, they think, feel, and behave pretty much as they would even if they were not Christian. They answer "Christian" when asked, not because it makes any significant difference to them on a personal level, but simply because this religious identification is part of the cultural air they breath.

On one level, there's nothing wrong with this. Every society needs some sort of shared vision of the world and shared values to stay healthy. And, as the decline of communism suggests, it is difficult to support this shared vision and these shared values without some religious underpinnings. Civil religion is good, if not necessary, for a healthy culture.

Problems arise, however, when kingdom people fail to see that civil religion is simply an aspect of the kingdom of the world. Problems arise when kingdom people forget that the kingdom of God always looks like Jesus and so has no intrinsic relationship with *any* civil religion. Problems arise when we fail to see that the civil religion of Christianity has no more kingdom-of-God significance than the civil religion of Buddhism, Hinduism, or the ancient Roman Pantheon.

THE HARMFUL ILLUSION OF THE CIVIL RELIGION

When we fail to distinguish between the quasi-Christian civil religion of America and the kingdom of God, two things happen.

First, American kingdom people lose their missionary zeal. Because we buy the myth that we live in a Christian nation, as defined by the civil religion, we don't live with the same missionary zeal we'd have if we lived, say, in a country where Buddhism or Hinduism was the civil religion. This is why American Christians so often define "missions" as sending people to *other* countries—as though there was more missionary work to do *there* than *here*.

I believe this sentiment is rooted in an illusion. If you peel back the façade of the civil religion, you find that America is about as pagan as any country we could ever send missionaries to. Despite what a majority of Americans say when asked by pollsters, we are arguably no less self-centered, unethical, or prone toward violence than most other cultures. We generally look no more like Jesus, dying on a cross out of love for the people who crucified him, than do people in other cultures, and thus are generally no closer to the kingdom of God than people in other cultures. The fact that we have a quasi-Christian civil religion doesn't help; if anything, it hurts precisely because it creates the illusion in the minds of kingdom people that we are closer to the example of Jesus than we actually are (cf. Matt. 21:31).

If we simply hold fast to the truth that the kingdom of God always looks like Jesus, we can see the irrelevance, if not harmfulness, of the quasi-Christian civil religion for the advancement of the kingdom of God. When a kingdom person realizes that the civil religion of America has no more relationship to the real kingdom of God than any other civil religion—that it's all just part of the religious trappings most versions of the kingdom of the world adopt—they are motivated to live as much as a missionary in

America as they would if they were stationed in, say, China, Cambodia, or India. The only significant difference is that in at least one respect it's arguably *harder* to be a missionary in America, for here the majority think they're already Christian simply by virtue of living in a Christian nation. Their need for the true kingdom is concealed behind a civil surrogate of the kingdom.[7]

THE DISTRACTION OF THE CIVIL RELIGION

A second thing that happens when we fail to distinguish the civil religion of America from the kingdom of God is that we end up wasting precious time and resources defending and tweaking the civil religion—as though doing so had some kingdom value. We strive to keep prayer in the schools, fight for the right to have public prayer before football games, lobby to preserve the phrases "under God" in our Pledge of Allegiance and "in God we trust" on our coins, battle to hold the traditional civil meaning of marriage, and things of the sort—as though winning these fights somehow brings America closer to the kingdom of God. This, we think, is part of what it means to "take America back for God."

Now, you may or may not agree that preserving the civil religion in this way is good for the culture. Vote your conscience. But can we really believe that tweaking civil religion in these ways actually brings people closer to the kingdom of God, that it helps them become more like Jesus? For example, does anyone really think that allowing for a prayer before social functions is going to help students become kingdom people? Might not such prayer—and the political efforts to defend such prayer—actually be harmful to the kingdom inasmuch as it reinforces the shallow civil religious mindset that sees prayer primarily as a perfunctory religious activity? Might it not be better to teach our kids that true kingdom prayer has nothing to do with perfunctory social functions, that true kingdom prayer cannot be demanded or retracted by social laws and that their job as kingdom warriors is to "pray without ceasing" (1 Thess. 5:17) whether the law allows for it to be publicly expressed or not?

In other words, rather than spending time and energy defending and tweaking the civil religion, might it not be in the best interest of the kingdom of God to *distance* ourselves from the civil religion? Couldn't one even go so far as to argue that it would be good for the kingdom of God if this civic brand of pseudo-Christianity died altogether? Isn't one of the primary problems we're up against in this nation the fact that Christianity has been trivialized by being associated with civic functions? And aren't we actually reinforcing this trivialization by fighting so vigorously to preserve this pseudo-Christian veneer? Maybe Kierkegaard was right when he stated that the worst form of apostasy the Christian faith can undergo is to have it become simply an aspect of a culture.[8] Perhaps it would be a benefit to the advancement of this kingdom if America *looked* as pagan as it actually is, if the word *God* wasn't so trivially sprinkled on our coins, our Pledge of Allegiance, our civic functions, and elsewhere. Then perhaps the word might come to mean something significant to people who genuinely hunger and thirst for the real thing!

When the public stance of Christians is associated with preserving and tweaking the civil religion, we reinforce the impression that Christianity is primarily about the civil religion, about engaging in social functions, answering a pollster a certain way, and perhaps performing "religious obligations" a couple times of year by going to church and giving a couple of dollars. Would it not be better if kingdom people spent their time and energy doing authentic kingdom things—that is, *looking like Jesus*? Would it not be beneficial if we individually and corporately dedicated ourselves to serving others in Christlike love?

WHAT IF WE DID THE KINGDOM?

What if the energy and resources used to preserve and tweak the civil religion was rather spent feeding the hungry, housing the homeless, befriending the drug addict, and visiting the prisoner? What if our focus was on sacrificing our resources to help inner-city schools and safety houses for battered women? What if our concern was to bridge the ungodly racial gap in our country by developing friendships and collaborating in endeavors with people whose ethnicity is different than our own? What if instead of trying to defend our religious rights, Christians concerned themselves with siding with others whose rights are routinely trampled? What if instead of trying to legally make life more difficult for gays, we worried only about how we could affirm their unsurpassable worth in service to them?

In other words, what if we individually and collectively committed ourselves to the one thing that is needful—to replicating the loving sacrifice of Calvary to all people, at all times, in all places, regardless of their circumstances or merit? What if we just *did* the kingdom?

This is far more difficult than merely protecting the civil religion, which perhaps partly explains why so many prefer focusing on the civil religion. *Doing* the kingdom always requires that we bleed for others, and for just this reason, *doing* the kingdom accomplishes something kingdom-of-the-world activity can never accomplish. It may not immediately adjust people's behavior, but this is not what it seeks to accomplish. Rather, it transforms people's hearts and therefore transforms society.

FORGETTING THE "POWER UNDER" OF PRAYER

We have seen that buying into the myth of a Christian nation harms not only global missions but missions in America as well. A third damaging aspect concerns the effect the myth has on kingdom people in terms of what power they tend to trust. If we think that our nation is Christian—or at least close to being Christian—then it makes sense that we who take the Christian faith most seriously need to gain more of Caesar's "basically Christian" power to enforce a more "Christian" way of living. We would obviously never think this way if we were missionaries in, say, China. We succumb to this Constantinian temptation only because we mistakenly think that America, as opposed to China, is already "basically Christian."

As a result, many Americans place exaggerated confidence in the ability of Christians to influence society by political means rather than by distinctly kingdom-of-God means. What are distinctly kingdom-of-God means of influencing society? The answer, as always, is found by looking at Jesus.

Among other things, Jesus set an example for us to follow by being a person who consistently prayed (Matt. 26:36; Luke 5:16; 6:12; 9:28; 11:1). Not surprisingly, the New Testament reinforces this example by instructing kingdom citizens to be people of persistent prayer (Luke 6:28; 11:5–8; 18:1–6; Eph. 6:18; 1 Thess. 5:17; 1 Tim. 2:8; James 5:14). This is one means of influence we are to place our trust in, and so intercessory prayer—a distinctly kingdom-of-God form of social action—is one of our primary sacrificial acts of service to the world. As kingdom people, we have a unique authority and responsibility to affect what comes to pass by calling on God, and we are to use this authority in service to others.[9] It's one of the primary ways we exercise "power under" others.

Both the Old and the New Testaments emphasize the power and urgency of prayer. In fact, dozens of times the Bible depicts the fate of a nation as hanging in the balance not on what society did or on what politicians did, but on whether or not the people of God prayed.

To give one example, the Lord told Ezekiel that because the leaders of Israel were acting unjustly, oppressing "the poor and needy," he was going to bring judgment on the land (Ezek. 22:29). Yet he "sought for anyone among them who would repair the wall and stand in the breach ... on behalf of the land"—someone who would pray—in which case he "would not destroy it." Unfortunately, the Lord "found no one." "Therefore," he told Ezekiel, "I have poured out my indignation upon them" (Ezek. 22:30–31).

What a revealing passage! Despite its unjust practices, the land would have been spared had the Lord found an intercessor. A number of times in Scripture the prayer of one or more people altered God's plan and thus altered the course of history (e.g., Ex. 32:10–14; Deut. 9:13–29; 1 Kings 21:21–29).[10]

Dare we accept the obvious implications of this passage in Ezekiel? Dare we believe that the primary thing that may affect what happens in and to a nation is not what politicians do behind closed doors, but what kingdom people do—or don't do—on their knees in their prayer closets (Matt. 6:6)? Dare we accept that it's not primarily the righteousness or sinfulness of a nation that determines whether God blesses or curses it, but the presence or absence of prayer on the part of those who call themselves his people?

When the 9/11 attacks occurred, a number of evangelical spokespeople pointed the finger at the ACLU, gay-rights lobbyists, and other typical evangelical scapegoats—despite the New Testament's repeated insistence that we are not to judge others (Matt. 7:1–5; Rom. 2:1–3; 14:2–3, 10–13; James 4:10–12). Because of the sin of these people, it was suggested, God's "hand of protection" had been lifted off our nation.

According to Jesus, however, the whole business of trying to discern the hand of God in catastrophic events—just as a psychic might read tea leaves—is misguided (Luke 13:1–5). But blaming others for tragic events is even worse! If we took Ezekiel 22 seriously, our inclination would not be to judge others, but to assume responsibility ourselves. Whatever sin might exist in the ACLU, among gay-rights lobbyists, and others, we who are citizens of the kingdom of God must assume it to be a mere dust particle compared to the tree trunk of sin that protrudes out of our own eyes (Matt. 7:1–5). And whatever else our tree trunk includes, it includes the sin of not praying enough for others and for our nation. Were the people of God judging less and praying more, who knows but that this tragedy might have been lessened or avoided altogether? Who knows?

Why do we not place more trust in the power of prayer to affect the world? One primary reason, I think, is our national myth. Because we think our nation is "basically Christian," we tend to trust Caesar's "basically Christian" power more than Christ's. We therefore allow ourselves to be sucked into the "power over" game of politics, thinking that if only we can pass certain laws and enact certain policies, the Christian status of our nation will be improved. While we, of course, tip our hat to the need for prayer, our actions belie the fact that we generally (there *are* marvelous exceptions!) place more confidence in our individual and corporate political activity than we do in the power of prayer.

As U.S. citizens we have a civil right to influence the political system. But in following our consciences, we must never forget where our *real* power—our distinctly kingdom power—lies. It's not in "power over" but in "power under." It's not the power of your vote—every citizen of a democratic country has this; it's the power of your kingdom heart expressed on your knees in loving service to the world.

We will only be motivated to live this out consistently if we understand that the power of Caesar is not and never can be a distinctly kingdom-of-God power. Hence, the urgency for us to exercise the unique kingdom power of prayer is the same for kingdom people in America as it is for those in North Vietnam, China, or India. The kingdom of God always looks like Jesus wherever and whenever it appears.

SOCIAL ACTIVISM JESUS STYLE

The myth that America is a Christian nation causes us to minimize a second, distinctly kingdom way of influencing society. Many are so conditioned by the "power over" mindset of the world that they can't even envision an alternative way of affecting society and politics other than by playing the political game. Some thus conclude that, since Jesus didn't try to overhaul the political systems of his day by political means, the Christian faith must be reduced to private piety without any social relevance. This is an especially prevalent assumption among upper-middle-class, white evangelicals who often don't notice how the white-dominated power structures of society privilege them while oppressing others. In reality, however, nothing could be further from the truth!

As John Howard Yoder has brilliantly shown in his book *The Politics of Jesus*, everything about Jesus' ministry was socially and politically relevant.[11] Precisely because he did not allow the society or the politics of his day to define his ministry, he positioned himself to make a revolutionary prophetic comment, and ultimately have revolutionary impact on the society and politics of his day.

Jesus didn't buy into the limited options the culture placed before him. He rather exposed ugly injustices in all kingdom-of-the-world options by offering a radically distinct alternative. It is a kingdom that resists the demonic pull toward "power over" violence that characterizes all versions of the kingdom of the world. It is, therefore, a kingdom that, through self-sacrifice, unmasks the ugly injustice and violence of all versions of the kingdom of the world and the demonic powers that fuel them. It is a kingdom that doesn't wage war "against flesh and blood" but instead fights against "rulers, against the authorities, against the cosmic powers of this present darkness" (Eph. 6:12) that hold all people, oppressor and oppressed, in bondage.[12] It is a beautiful kingdom that is not so much spoken as it is displayed in loving action.

For example, Jesus never entered into the fray of particular debates about the status of women in society. He rather exposed the ugliness of patriarchalism by the countercultural way he treated women. Ignoring negative consequences for his reputation—and ultimately for his life—Jesus befriended them and gave them a culturally unprecedented dignity. In a society in which women were generally understood to be the property of men and in which women had few rights, Jesus' actions were revolutionary. While the mustard seed of the kingdom continues to grow slowly, Jesus' life established that in the kingdom community men and women would be regarded as equals (Gal. 3:26–29). As such, it provides a beautiful alternative to the male-dominated kingdom of the world and exposes the ugly injustices of this present world system in the process.

The same may be said of Jesus' treatment of social outcasts. His beautiful service to lepers, the blind, the demonized, the poor, prostitutes, and tax collectors screamed volumes about the inhumanity of various first-century social taboos and laws. While the mustard seed of the kingdom continues to grow slowly, Jesus' life established that in the kingdom community no distinction would be made on the basis of a person's social, economic, moral, or even religious standing. As such, it provides a beautiful alternative to the sociopolitical structures of the world and exposes the injustices of these structures in the process.

Along these same lines, Jesus exposed the inhumanity of certain religious rules (which in first-century Judaism had political force) by healing and feeding people on the Sabbath. And he exposed the evil of racial prejudice by fellowshipping with Samaritans and Gentiles and placing them in praiseworthy positions in his teachings (e.g., Luke 10:29–37; 17:11–19; John 4:4–39; cf. Matt. 8:5–10). While the mustard seed grows slowly, Jesus' life established that in the kingdom community people would be placed above rules and walls of racism would be torn down. As such, Jesus' kingdom provides a beautiful alternative to the socioreligious structures of the world and exposes the inhumanity and racist dimension of these structures in the process.

Finally, and most fundamentally, Jesus exposed the barbarism of the Roman government, and ultimately the barbarism of all "power over" kingdoms, by allowing himself to be crucified by them. Instead of using the power available to him to preserve his life, he exercised the power of love by giving his life for the very people who were taking it. While the mustard seed continues to grow slowly, Jesus' death established that the kingdom community would not be characterized by "power over" but by "power under." It would be a community where people have the same attitude as Jesus and thus place other people's interests above their own (Phil.

2:4–5; cf. Rom. 15:1–2; Gal. 6:2; James 2:15–16; 1 John 3:14–18). It would be a community that looked like him, for it would be a community of people who "live in love, as Christ loved [them] and gave himself up for [them]" (Eph. 5:2). As such, Jesus' community provides a beautiful alternative to the "power over" structure of the world and exposes the self-centered ugliness of these structures in the process.

This is what we are called to be: a community characterized by radical, revolutionary, Calvary-quality love; a community that manifests the love of the triune God (John 17:21–26); a community that strives for justice not by conquering but by being willing to suffer; a community that God uses to transform the world by providing it with an alternative to its own self-centered, violent way of existing. How socially and politically revolutionary it would be if his disciples lived up to their calling!

AN EXAMPLE OF THE KINGDOM IN ACTION

A small illustration of how socially relevant and unique the kingdom of God in action can be may be helpful. A church I know committed itself to fixing up a dilapidated inner-city school. Government funding in their region had been drastically cut, and this church appropriately saw this as a marvelous kingdom opportunity. As they planned for and prayed about this project, word seeped out, and they began getting calls from local businesses and neighbors who wanted to help in the project, for kingdom beauty always attracts good-hearted people. Thousands upon thousands of dollars worth of food and materials for the workers were donated, and dozens of people from businesses and the surrounding neighborhood ended up joining the church in its work. With hundreds of people sacrificing time and energy, it took only ten hours for this school to undergo an "extreme makeover."

The kids who attended the school, the teachers who taught there, and the neighbors and businesses who participated in or witnessed this renovation were deeply impacted. A fragmented, economically disadvantaged community was drawn together, resulting in a school building they could all take pride in. A long-term relationship developed between this school and the church, with people from the church volunteering in and praying for the school on a regular basis. Even more fundamentally, people saw Calvary-quality love in action, and some of them began to wonder, "Why would these people do this for us?" *This* is the question the church ought to be continually raising in people's minds by its radical service to the world.[13]

Not only this, but the action caught the attention of certain people in the government. The beauty of this act called public attention to an ugly aspect of the region's social and political structure and forced the question, Why is there significant disparity between the conditions of and resources available to predominately white suburban schools, on the one hand, and predominately nonwhite, inner-city schools on the other? It poignantly raised the question of whether the officials who made the decision to cut funding in the first place really understood the negative impact their decision would make on these already disadvantaged students. The pressure put on government when the church lives in love, as Christ loved us and gave his life for us, must not be minimized.

JUST *DO* THE KINGDOM

Now, had that church decided to play the "power over" game of kingdom-of-the-world politics, it's unlikely the results would have been so positive. Had this church accepted the limited options given them by the kingdom of the world, the congregation would likely have divided between those who believe that the Republican economic approach is best and those who think the Democratic economic approach is best. Some might have sincerely thought that, given the totality of factors affecting the state's budget, cutting school funding was a necessary evil, while others might have sincerely concluded it was done only because the government immorally privileges the rich and powerful.

It's even possible the competing sides would have followed the common worldly practice of questioning the character of the opposing side. "If you *really* cared about these hurting kids," I can hear someone say, "you'd support the Democratic party." "If *you* really cared about helping these hurting kids," others may have responded, "you'd support the Republican party." And at that point there would be little hope of the "Matthews" and the "Simons" in this congregation and surrounding community working together to do the distinctly kingdom thing for this inner-city school.

Fortunately, instead of trying to arrive at the "right" kingdom-of-the-world approach to the problem this school faced, the church just decided to *do* the kingdom. Why should it rely on government—or any particular political party within government—to do the right thing? Why should the church confine itself to the limited options given by the political machinery of the culture? Instead of trusting "power over," why not trust "power under"? When this church did so, they discovered that the beauty of Calvary has a power to effect profound change on an individual, social, and political level.

The kingdom-of-God approach has more power than the ability to Christianize one of the limited package deals given by competing political groups. Providing a beautiful, Calvary-like alternative attracts people, unifies them, and calls attention to issues too easily ignored by the power structures of the world. It thereby impacts the social structures even while it advances the kingdom of God in the world.

AGAIN, WHAT IF WE JUST DID THE KINGDOM?

There are, thankfully, many beautiful example of congregations and organizations living out their radical kingdom lifestyle in America. But what would happen if kingdom people in general made it their sole concern to live like this—"in love, as Christ loved us and gave himself up for us"? What if we integrated this attitude into every area of our life and society?

Imagine, for example, what would happen if white kingdom people chose to reverse the white dominance of American culture and, in a variety of ways, placed themselves in service to nonwhites? What if white Christians entered into solidarity with nonwhites and made the struggles of nonwhites their own? What if they used their position of privilege not for their own gain but to help bring nonwhites up to their status? What if kingdom people didn't make themselves dependent on government to resolve racial tensions, but rather assumed responsibility to eradicate centuries of cultural racism in this country in their own lives, in the life of their own congregations, and in the lives of those in their community? What would happen if Christian individuals and entire congregations were intentional in proclaiming—with their lives—that a central reason Jesus died was to reverse Babel (Gen. 11) and to tear down walls of hostility between people (Eph. 2:14–16)?

Such Calvary-like activity would put on display a kingdom love and kingdom unity the world is not capable of and would, for this reason, advance the kingdom of God and attract people to Jesus Christ (John 17:20–26). The "power under" beauty of the kingdom would turn a spotlight on the ugly racism of American culture that is so easy for whites and, therefore, the white-dominated power structures to ignore. It would advance the kingdom of God even while it impacts the sociopolitical structures.

Of course, as American citizens, we can use our access to government to make the kingdom of the world as just as possible. How to best do this amid the ambiguity of the limited options presented by this version of the kingdom of the world is a difficult and controversial topic. But as kingdom-of-God citizens, we need not, and must not, wait for these issues to be resolved before we act. Our trust, time, energy, and resources must not be centered on improving government but on living out the revolutionary kingdom of Jesus Christ in every way, shape, and form. It must be centered on praying and bleeding for others; it must be centered on coming under others, especially (following Jesus' example) those who suffer at the hands of the kingdom of the world.

When we individually and corporately bleed for others, the kingdom of God is advanced, and we end up having an impact on individuals and on the sociopolitical systems we'd never have if we merely played the kingdom-of-the-world game on its own terms. Resisting the temptation for quick, "power over" solutions and choosing the more sacrificial, discrete "power under" approach of Jesus is difficult. But it alone has the power to unify the church, advance the kingdom, transform hearts, and thereby move society closer to the reign of God.

CHAPTER 7

WHEN CHIEF SINNERS BECOME MORAL GUARDIANS

Do not judge, so that you may not be judged.
Why do you see the speck in your neighbor's eye,
but do not notice the log in your own eye?
Or how can you say to your neighbor,
"Let me take the speck out of your eye,"
while the log is in your own eye?

MATTHEW 7:1, 3–4

WE HAVE DISCUSSED THE HARM THAT THE MYTH OF A CHRISTIAN NATION does to global missions, local missions, and the church's commitment to trust "power under" rather than "power over." Now we need to discuss a fourth damaging consequence.

As we've seen, when people who are serious about their Christian faith buy into the myth that America is a Christian nation, they can easily conclude that it is their job to keep America as Christian as possible, if not restore America back to its supposed Christian heritage. As a result, they may intentionally or unintentionally position themselves as moral guardians of society, coming to believe it is their job to preserve and promote moral issues — and fix moral problems. They sometimes believe themselves to be the moral conscience of the nation, keeping society from cutting the tether to its Christian heritage and spinning out of control. In their minds, it makes sense to play the role of moral guardian — after all, they know the Scripture and, thus, know God's will for society better than others.

While this view has been a basic assumption of a large portion of the American church throughout our history, I will argue that it is fundamentally misguided, even harmful to the advancement of the kingdom of God.

I believe there are at least five fundamental problems with this perspective.

THE EXAMPLE OF JESUS

First, as people called to mimic Jesus in every area of our lives, we should find it significant that Jesus never assumed the position of moral guardian over any individual, let alone over the culture at large. In his ministry, he never once inquired into a person's moral status. (In a moment we'll discuss his engagement with Jewish religious authorities.) While he certainly dealt with some disreputable people (e.g., John 4:5–29), never once did he judge them (John 8:15) or try to control their behavior. As the one sinless person in history, he was the only one who could have justifiably assumed a position of moral superiority over others; unlike the rest of us, he didn't have tree trunks sticking out of his own eyes (Matt. 7:1–5)! But remarkably, he never adopted this position.

Why didn't the sinless Jesus point out, condemn, and try to control people's morality? It certainly wasn't because people in his day were less sinful than they are today. By most reckonings, morality in Jesus' day was a good bit worse than it is today. While we may get upset over a president having a sexual liaison with a young intern, for example, Roman rulers routinely engaged in outrageous sexual escapades. Yet, while Jesus certainly didn't condone such behavior, we have no record of him so much as commenting on it. His purpose, apparently, was not to guard, promote, or fix public morality.

It is true that Jesus, as a Jewish prophet, publicly confronted the Jewish religious leadership for their hypocrisy in enslaving people in a shallow, legalistic religious system and using religion for their own monetary and social gain (Matt. 21:12–13; 23:13–36). But it's important to understand that this sort of activity fell in line with a long prophetic tradition among Jews, and that it was accepted as part of the Jewish, theocratic, covenantal self-understanding. A Jewish prophet was supposed to hold Jewish religious and political leaders accountable, but neither Jesus nor any other Jewish prophet tried to hold non-Jewish leaders accountable. Jesus' confrontations with the Jewish religious leaders is more comparable to a Catholic cardinal reprimanding parish priests for abusing their flock than it is to Christians trying to regulate the morality of their non-Christian culture.

The apostle Paul played a similar role within his congregations (e.g., 1 Cor. 5) and encouraged other pastors to do the same (e.g., 1 Tim. 5:20; 2 Tim. 4:2). In appropriate ecclesial contexts such as these—contexts in which people have entered into a covenantal relationship with a spiritual leader—confronting damaging behavior is sometimes necessary—and expected. Because the people being confronted have willingly placed themselves under the authority of the one doing the confronting, it is likely to be received as an expression of love and, thus, have positive results. Outside of such covenantal relationships, however, such confrontations would not likely be received as loving and not likely be beneficial. Indeed, such confrontations would be inappropriate, falling into the category of judgmentally looking for dust particles in people's eyes when they haven't invited you to do so (Matt. 7:1–3). This is why Paul explicitly said he had no business—and no interest in—judging those outside the church in the broader Corinthian community (1 Cor. 5:12). And note that he makes this statement in the very same context in which he reprimands his congregation for condoning outrageous sinful behavior within the body of Christ (1 Cor. 5:12–13).[1]

There is a place, then, for leaders to confront appropriately those who follow them and even for believers to play a role in confronting other believers (Matt. 18:15–18; Luke 17:3). But everything hangs on the context. First-century Christians met frequently—often daily—in each other's houses (Acts 2:46; Rom. 16:5; 1 Cor. 16:19; Col. 4:15; Philem. v. 2; 2 John 10; cf. Acts 8:3; 12:12). In a world that was often hostile toward them, they ate together, worshiped together, studied together, shared resources with one another, and lived life together in small house churches. In other words, they lived in intimate, covenantal relationships with one another. All the "one another's" in the New Testament presuppose this house-church context, and in covenantal contexts such as this—contexts in which everybody knows one another and knows they are loved by the others—confrontation is likely to be received as loving rather than as judgmental and is more likely to be beneficial to the person being confronted for just this reason.[2]

Outside of such contexts, however, such confrontations are inappropriate. They are, at best, rude—and love is never rude (1 Cor. 13:5). Hence, while Jesus played a religious, covenantal role in confronting the Pharisees and cleansing the temple, he never acted like this in his broader day-to-day ministry. Here, Jesus just met needs, no questions asked, and *this* is to be our model for ministry to the world at large.

Jesus encountered numerous demonized people but never once inquired what they might have done to come under such bondage. He encountered scores of afflicted people, but consistently resisted the age-old temptation to look for a moral explanation for their affliction (John 9:1–5; cf. Luke 13:1–5). He never performed a "background check" on those he served or those who followed him. When people were hungry, he fed them. When a wedding host ran out of wine, he made more wine. When prostitutes, tax collectors, and others judged to be "the worst" in society followed him around, he made himself available for friendship, no questions asked—and with no concern for his own reputation (Matt. 11:19; Luke 7:34; cf. Mark 2:15–16). The agenda he lived by, and the agenda he gave his disciples to live by, was to demonstrate the kingdom by serving people and then announcing that the kingdom had come (e.g., Luke 10:5–9).

TWO POSSIBLE EXCEPTIONS?

Despite this clear pattern, some try to justify their self-appointed role as society's moral guardians by citing Jesus' words to the woman caught in the act of adultery: "Go and sin no more" (John 8:11 KJV). Shouldn't we be standing up for social morality by telling people they should stop sinning?

We need to remember that it's one thing for a sinless person like Jesus to say "sin no more" and quite another for people like us—with tree trunks protruding out of our eyes—to say the same thing. But even more crucially, remember that the central point of this passage is that none of the woman's accusers was in a position to judge her—because they were as much sinners as she. Jesus invited whoever was without sin to cast the first stone—the prescribed punishment for adultery—but no one met this requirement (John 8:6–9). Meanwhile, the only one who could have justifiably cast the stone refused to. Jesus did not condemn this woman but rather told her to henceforth abstain from this sinful—and obviously dangerous—activity. One lesson of the passage is this: if you want to judge someone else, you first have to be sinless. Of course, if you are sinless, like Jesus, you won't have any inclination to do so.

Another episode from John is sometimes used to justify Christians assuming moral guardianship over others. Jesus pointed out to the Samaritan woman he met at the well that she had had five husbands and was now living with a man who was not her husband (John 4:16–18).

True enough, but it's again important to look at the context. Jesus didn't mention this information to confront, judge, or fix this woman. Though he alludes to her past, he offers no commentary on it, and having alluded to it, he drops it as irrelevant to his primary concern. The only reason he let this woman know that he was aware of her unsavory past was to convince her that he was the Messiah, and that if this woman would "drink" the water he had to offer she would never thirst again. He was letting this woman know that he knew everything about her past—and yet the offer of "life" was still on the table, no questions asked! This is why the woman went back to her town joyfully proclaiming that she'd met a man who knew everything about her—including her sin (John 4:29). Had there been any shame or judgment involved, meeting a man who knew everything about her would hardly have been a joyful encounter.

We don't know what became of this woman. Was she convicted of her sin? Did she move out of the house of the man she was living with? Did she marry him? Did she finally get her moral act together? We don't know, for the point of the story is not how Jesus fixes people's moral lives but how he loves people and offers them everlasting life as they are, regardless of their moral lives. Whatever transforming impact God's love has on people, it has incredible power because it is given before—and apart from—the transformation itself.

This is how we are called to love. We are to be the shadow that Jesus casts—to imitate God by "living in love, as Christ loved us and gave himself up for us" (Eph. 5:2). We are to demonstrate the kingdom by Calvary-quality acts of service and then proclaim that the domain in which God is king has come. We are to see a need and meet it—no questions asked. We are to love even our enemies with an unconditional, nonjudgmental love, and, thereby, offer everlasting life to all who are thirsty. To do this means we must refrain from doing what Jesus never did: namely, positioning ourselves as wiser, morally superior guardians and "fixers" of others. Moral guardianship is what the Pharisees did—not Jesus.

THOU SHALL NOT JUDGE

Second, when we assume the role of moral guardians of the culture, we invariably position ourselves as judges over others. Not only is there no precedent for this in the life of Jesus, but Scripture explicitly and repeatedly forbids us to judge others.

For example, immediately after telling us (twice) to love our enemies (Luke 6:27, 35), Jesus says, "Do not judge, and you will not be judged; do not condemn, and you will not be condemned" (Luke 6:37). Jesus contrasts love and judgment as antithetical activities; we can't do both at the same time. This is why the original sin of the Bible is depicted as eating from "the tree of the knowledge of good and evil" (Gen. 2:9, 17; 3:5, 22).[3] Our fundamental job is to love like God loves, not to pretend that we know what only God knows. For unlike God, we can't do the former so long as we're trying to do the latter.

So too Paul says that when we judge others we are passing judgment on ourselves, for we are as guilty as any we would care to judge (Rom. 2:1). James says that when we judge we are acting like God himself. "There is one lawgiver and judge who is able to save and to destroy," he says. "So who, then, are you to judge your neighbor?" (James 4:12).

This applies especially to the way Christians view those yet outside the kingdom community. As we noted above, while Paul acknowledges a role Christian leaders must play in discerning and correcting behavior within their congregations, he denied he had any right, ability, or interest in judging "those outside [the church]" (1 Cor. 5:12). Like Jesus, no part of Paul's kingdom ministry involved trying to tweak the morality of the culture at large. Like Jesus, his only concern was that kingdom people consistently live out the new life they have within the kingdom, for only when they do this will they offer the culture at large a beautiful, kingdom alternative to their present, sinful, self-centered, and, ultimately, destructive way of living.

AN UGLY REPUTATION

Third, and closely related to this, when the church sets itself up as the moral police of the culture, we earn the reputation of being self-righteous judgers rather than loving, self-sacrificial servants—the one reputation we are called to have. While tax collectors and prostitutes gravitated to Jesus because of his magnetic kingdom love, these sorts of sinners steer clear of the church, just as they did the Pharisees, and for the exact same reasons: they do not experience unconditional love and acceptance in our midst—they experience judgment.

The brutal fact is that we Christians are not generally known for our love—for the simple reason that we, like the Pharisees of old, generally judge more than we love. Ask any random sampling of pagans in America what first comes to their mind when you say the words *evangelical* or *born again* Christian, and chances are close to zero that anything like "outrageous, sacrificial love" will be the first thing out of their mouths. Ask them to list the first ten things that come into their mind, and chances are still close to zero that "outrageous, sacrificial love" will be on any of their lists. Indeed, a recent survey demonstrated that, when asked to rank people groups in terms of their respectability, "evangelical Christians" were ranked one notch above the bottom, just above prostitutes.[4]

This is nothing short of catastrophic! Love is the all-or-nothing of the kingdom of God. *Above all* we are to love (Col. 3:14; 1 Peter 4:8). *Everything* we do is to be done in love and, thus, communicate love (1 Cor. 16:14). We are to imitate God by living in Christlike love (Eph. 5:1–2), and if we do this, we fulfill the whole law (Matt. 22:37–40; Rom. 13:8–10). If we lack this, everything else we do is devoid of kingdom value, however impressive it might otherwise be (1 Cor. 13:1–3). Not only this, but God has leveraged the expansion of his kingdom on the church loving like Christ loves (John 13:35; 17:20–26). By God's own design, the corporate "body of Christ" is to grow as the corporate body does exactly what the incarnate body of Christ did—dying for those who crucified him.

For the church to lack love is for the church to lack *everything*. No heresy could conceivably be worse!

Despite our widespread reputation, of course, we evangelical Christians often insist that we *are* loving; it's just that the world is so sinful they can't see it—or so we tell ourselves. *They* don't understand what "true love" is. That attitude is frankly as arrogant as it is tragic. People in the first century were not less sinful than people in the twenty-first, yet God expected to win first-century people by the sheer beauty of Christ's love shining on Calvary and radiating through his corporate body. Why think anything has changed? If contemporary people don't see in us what ancient people saw in Christ, it can only be because the love that was present in Christ *isn't* present in us. And if they see in us what they saw in ancient

Pharisees, it can only be because the self-righteousness found in the Pharisees *is* found in us.

Our comical insistence that we *are* loving, despite our reputation, is a bit like a man insisting he's a perfectly loving husband when his wife, kids, and all who know him insist he's an unloving, self-righteous jerk. If he persists in his self-serving opinion of himself, insisting that his wife, kids, and all who know him don't understand what "true love" is, it simply confirms the perspective these others have of him. This, I submit, is precisely the position much of the evangelical church of America is in. Until the culture at large instinctively identifies us as loving, humble servants, and until the tax collectors and prostitutes of our day are beating down our doors to hang out with us as they did with Jesus, we have every reason to accept our culture's judgment of us as correct. We are indeed more pharisaic than we are Christlike.

If we would simply internalize Jesus' teaching that we are to consider our own sin to be tree trunks in our eyes and other people's sin—whatever it is—to be a mere dust particle, we would quickly become known not as self-righteous judgers but as the most humble, self-effacing people on the planet. Paul's cry will be our cry: "We are the worst of sinners" (see 1 Tim. 1:15). If we would combine this humility with a resolve to simply love as Jesus loved—love as we have been loved by Christ—we would become known as a people who make no claim for themselves, but who simply live to serve others. We are slaves of Jesus Christ (Eph. 6:6); we are slaves to a love that compels us (2 Cor. 5:14). And because of this, we are humble servants of humanity.

While the ugliness of self-serving, judgmental religion pushes people away from the kingdom, the beauty of humble, Calvary-quality love pulls them in. If we lived in love as Christ loved us and gave himself for us, we would in time possibly find tax collectors and prostitutes hanging out with us, just as they did Jesus. For only in a kingdom context such as this can they experience an unconditional love, worth, and acceptance they can't find anywhere else.

THE HYPOCRISY OF OUR JUDGMENT

Fourth, when people assume the position of moral guardians of the culture, they invite—they *earn*!—the charge of hypocrisy. For all judgment, save the judgment of the omniscient and holy God, involves hypocrisy. Whenever we "eat of the tree of the knowledge of good and evil"—that is, whenever we find some element of worth, significance, and purpose in contrasting ourselves as "good" with others we deem "evil"—we do so in a self-serving and selective manner. We always bend the tree, as it were, to our own advantage and, as a result, we do the exact opposite of what Jesus taught us to do. Instead of seeing our own sins as worse than others, we invariably set up a list of sins in which *our* sins are deemed minor while *other people's* sins are deemed major. We may have dust particles in our eyes, we reason, but at least we don't have tree trunks like "*those* people." Unlike the tax collector who made no moral claims for himself, we thank the Lord we are not like other people just as the Pharisee did (Luke 18:9–14).

Our grading of sins has nothing to do with Scripture, of course, for Scripture not only has no such graded list of sins; it specifically teaches against such a notion. A major point of Jesus' teaching was to lop us all off at the knees on the sin issue. As it concerns our standing before God, the person who insults someone once is in as dire a spot as the serial killer (Matt. 5:21–22). No, our graded sin lists have nothing to do with Scripture but are rather rooted in a fallen but primal need to feel secure in our own righteousness. However imperfect we may be, we want to believe that we are not as bad as others.

We feed our self-righteousness with this illusory contrast by ascribing ourselves worth at the expense of others. But "the others" we feed off of see the self-serving hypocrisy of the self-righteous and self-serving exercise, even if we don't.

To illustrate, more than a few have noticed the comic irony in the fact that the group most vocal about "the sanctity of marriage," namely evangelical Christians, happens to be the group with the highest number of divorces in the United States, which itself has the highest divorce rate in the world![5] Numerous explanations have been offered by Christians to minimize this embarrassment, but none of them are convincing—or even relevant. Whatever our excuses, outsiders legitimately wonder, "If evangelicals want to enforce by law the 'the sanctity of marriage,' why don't they try to outlaw divorce and remarriage? Better yet, why don't they stop worrying about laws to regulate *others'* behavior and spend their time and energy sanctifying their *own* marriages?"

Do evangelicals fear gay marriage in particular because the Bible is much more clear about the wrongfulness of gay marriage than it is about the wrongfulness of divorce and remarriage? No, for the Bible actually says a good deal more against divorce and remarriage than it does against monogamous gay relationships. Do they go after this particular sin because the research shows that gay marriage is more damaging to society than divorce and remarriage? It seems not, for while one might grant that neither is ideal, there's no clear evidence that the former is socially more harmful than the latter—especially given the fact that divorce and remarriage is far more widespread than gay marriage. But in any case, this point is completely irrelevant since the present issue isn't over gay *unions*. The issue is only over whether these unions should be called "marriages." To the best of my knowledge, no one has shown that the social welfare of our nation is significantly harmed by what monogamous gay unions are *called*.

Why then are so many evangelicals publicly obsessed with cracking down on this particular sin? There are undoubtedly a number of reasons, not least of which is that the loss of the traditional definition of marriage is a poignantly symbolic indication that the quasi-Christian civil religion of America is on the wane. And as we've said, many evangelicals believe that preserving and recovering this civil religion is their central kingdom duty. Whatever the reasons, however, outsiders have the impression that evangelicals go after this sin because it's one they don't generally have.

We evangelicals may be divorced and remarried several times; we may be as greedy and as unconcerned about the poor and as gluttonous as others in our culture; we may be as prone to gossip and slander and as blindly prejudiced as others in our culture; we may be more self-righteous and as rude as others in our culture—we may even lack love more than others in the culture. These sins are among the most frequently mentioned sins in the Bible. But at least we're not *gay*!

So despite the paucity of references to homosexuality relative to the sins we minimize or ignore, and despite empirical evidence that some of the sins we minimize are far more harmful to people and to society than this sin (for instance, greed and gluttony arguably kill millions!), *this* is the sin evangelicals as a group have decided to take a public stand on. Why? Because by drawing a line in the sand on this point we can feel that we're doing something righteous. We're standing up for truth and godliness; we're defending "God and country"; we're playing the role of moral guardian that (we believe) God has called us to play.[6]

Tragically, the self-serving and hypocritical nature of this moral posturing is apparent to nearly everyone—except those who do the posturing. And just as tragically, it causes multitudes to want nothing to do with the good news we have to offer. While the church was supposed to be the central means by which people became convinced that Jesus is for real, activity like this has made the church into the central reason many are convinced he's *not* for real. If I had ten dollars for every time I've encountered someone who resisted submitting to Christ simply because they "can't stand Christians," I'd have a fairly robust bank account.

There's nothing beautiful or attractive about this sort of self-serving, hypocritical behavior. The beauty of the cross and the magnetic quality of Calvary-quality love has been smothered in a blanket of self-righteous, self-serving, moralistic posturing.

To be clear, I'm not suggesting that the church should publicly take a stand *for* gay marriage, nor am I trying to influence how evangelicals vote. Some may feel it best for society to outlaw gay marriages—others to allow it. In a democracy you're asked to give your opinion on such matters, so give it according to your conscience. I'm simply maintaining that, in our role as public representatives of the kingdom of God, Christians should stick to replicating Calvary toward gay people (as toward all people), and trust that their loving service will do more to transform people than laws ever could.

If your particular burden is to free people from their homosexuality, then go about it in a Calvary-like fashion. Commit to suspending judgment, start befriending gays, and then serve them in love—for years. Perhaps your loving kindness will lead some of them to faith and open doors for dialogue as God gently works in their lives—just as he works in yours. You may eventually develop a trusting, committed relationship in which you are invited to address issues in a gay person's life as you invite them to address issues in your life, for God uses relationships like this to lead us all into greater conformity to Jesus Christ.

OUR INCOMPETENCE AS MORAL GUARDIANS

The fifth fundamental problem with the church being the moral guardian of society is that, throughout history, the church has proven itself to be a very poor moral guardian. As we noted in chapter 4, whenever the church exercises the power of Caesar to enforce its doctrine and convictions, the result has usually been at least as bad as any non-Christian version of the kingdom of the world. Even more concerning, it's been far more damaging to the kingdom of God than any other version of the kingdom of the world—precisely because in this instance the name of Christ was associated with the result.

There is no indication that the church is better qualified for the position of moral guardian today than it has been in the past. Not only have we not earned the right to be heard by consistently coming under others in love, but the arbitrary way many evangelicals seem to decide what needs addressing and what doesn't undermines our credibility as moral spokespeople. The fact that many evangelicals are publicly more upset about gay marriage than about divorce and remarriage, greed, gluttony, violence, and many other things is a case in point. But the arbitrariness can be extended much further.

For example, several days before the 2004 Super Bowl, a friend of mine who works with people in extreme poverty, including the dangerous ministry of rescuing children from forced prostitution, came back to the U.S. from Cambodia. On the night he returned to the U.S., he happened to catch a special that aired on television exposing the tragedy of childhood prostitution in Cambodia and Thailand, the very area where he works. The show accurately reported that approximately thirty thousand children are at any given time sold into sexual slavery in the region and that this business is financed primarily by Western "clients." I too along with several million others, saw this documentary and found it a horrifying, gut-wrenching presentation. There was, however, no public reaction on the part of evangelical Christians.

A few days later my friend watched the infamous Super Bowl in which Janet Jackson exposed her breast for several seconds during the halftime show. *This* caused Christians to react! The moralistic outcry was heard around the nation—for weeks. Through email, radio, magazines, pulpits, and a variety of other venues, individuals and congregations were urged to call their senators, boycott the stations and the products that support these stations, write letters to station managers and the FCC, and so on.

Of course, my friend too finds Janet Jackson's behavior juvenile and disgusting. What drove him to despair, however, was the fact that Christians seemed far more upset by a breast exposed for five seconds than by thirty thousand kids sold into sexual slavery. He and others justifiably wonder about the viability of the evangelical moral compass. Granted, many more watched the Super Bowl than watched the documentary on child sexual slavery, but this is really beside the point. Had Janet Jackson exposed her breast on the TV special rather than the Super Bowl, it would certainly have elicited much more of a reaction than the facts about childhood sexual slavery elicited.

This is hardly an isolated case, which leads many people to view the moral compass of the evangelical church, as a whole, to be quite bizarre. Issues related to sex get massive amounts of attention while issues related to corporate greed, societal greed, homelessness, poverty, racism, the environment, racial injustice, genocide, war, and the treatment of animals (the original divine mandate given to humans in Gen. 1:28) typically get little attention. Going into the sociological explanation for this odd prioritization would take us outside the scope of this work, but the fact that it exists calls into question the credibility of the evangelical church to be any kind of moral guardian. When evangelicals assume the posture of knowing what is best for society, it only serves to further undermine the credibility of the good news we are commissioned to proclaim, and it hinders the advancement of the kingdom of God.

Does this mean that evangelical Christians shouldn't speak out publicly on moral issues? Absolutely not! We should speak out, but we should do so in a distinctly kingdom way. We should speak with self-sacrificial actions more than with words. We should speak not as moral superiors but as self-confessing moral inferiors. We should call attention to issues by entering into solidarity with those who suffer injustice. We should seek to free people from sin by serving them, not by trying to lord it over them. And we should trust that God will use our Calvary-like service to others to advance his kingdom in the world.

Again, as citizens of a free country who are invited to give our opinions, we may enter the fray of conflicting political opinions as we see fit. But as public representatives of the kingdom of God, our confidence is to lie solely in God's promise to build his kingdom through Jesus' Spirit at work in and through us. This is where our focus must be, and this is what we must be willing to bleed for.

A KINGDOM APPROACH TO ABORTION

To illustrate, consider the highly charged and divisive issue of abortion. Whether one should vote pro-life or pro-choice is clearly an important question for all citizens to consider. Because all kingdom-of-the-world issues come in complex political packages, numerous complex considerations will affect how one votes on this issue.

There are, of course, many difficult metaphysical and ethical questions to consider. When does the fetus become a full person? When does it acquire a soul and take on the image of God?[7] Your answer to these questions will affect, and be affected by, your views on a host of other ethical questions. For example, do you believe that the morning-after pill is as bad as partial-birth abortions? Would your ideal society punish women who use the morning-after pill as severely as people who murder infants or adults? How should we weigh the rights of the unborn at various stages of development against the rights of the woman whose body it now inhabits? And to what extent do you believe government should legislate the answer to these questions as opposed to leaving the answer up to the woman and others involved in the pregnancy?

Related to these questions are a host of other complex considerations that will affect how you vote. For example, how does the party or candidate that most closely reflects your view on abortion fare on other issues you deem important: concern for the poor, economics, foreign affairs, war, the environment, and so on? How much weight do you put on each of these convictions? Also, what do you deem attainable at the present time in our culture? Is it more efficient to work to outlaw abortion outright, or is it better to minimize abortion by, say, voting for the candidate and party you think will best help the poor, since there is a demonstrable link between the rate of poverty and the rate of abortion in the U.S.? Even more fundamentally, do you think it more efficient to hold an uncompromising stance on this issue, or is it better for the unborn, and for society as a whole, for you to work with people who have different beliefs than yours to overcome our present polarization and find a middle ground? What do you believe is the best way to create a culture in which abortions are as unnecessary and rare as possible?

How one answers all these difficult and important questions affects how they vote. But kingdom people need to understand that *none* of these questions are distinctly kingdom questions. The polarized way the issue is framed in contemporary politics is largely a function of various groups trying to gain power over each other for what they believe to be the good of the whole, and while we as Americans have to consider these questions before we can give an informed opinion (a vote) when asked, there's no reason we—as kingdom-of-God participants—should allow this political way of framing the issue to define our approach. Jesus never allowed himself to be defined by the political conflicts of his day, and neither should we.

The distinctly kingdom question is not, How should we *vote*? The distinctly kingdom question is, How should we *live*? How can we individually and collectively come under women struggling with unwanted pregnancies and come under the unborn babies who are unwanted? How can we who are worse sinners than any woman with an unwanted pregnancy—and thus have no right to stand over them in judgment—sacrifice our time, energy, and resources to ascribe unsurpassable worth to them and their unborn children? How can we act in such a way that we communicate our agreement with Jesus that these women and their unborn children are worth dying for? How can we individually and collectively sacrifice for and serve women and their unwanted children so that it becomes feasible for the mother to go to full term? How can we individually and collectively bleed for pregnant women and for unborn babies in a way that maximizes life and minimizes violence?

We answer these distinctly kingdom questions not with our votes but with our *lives*. And, note, we don't need to answer any of the world's difficult political and metaphysical questions to do it. The unique kingdom approach to abortion isn't dependent on convincing ourselves and others that we have "God's knowledge" about highly ambiguous questions. It's based on our call to love as Jesus loved. There's a scared woman; there's a growing life inside her, which, however it got there and whatever speculations one holds about its metaphysical status, is a miraculous creation of God. And the only relevant question kingdom people need to answer is, Are we willing to bleed for *both*?

Voting and picketing costs us little. The kingdom approach costs us much. But it is precisely the costliness of the kingdom approach—which looks like Jesus dying on Calvary for those who crucified him—that makes it a unique *kingdom* approach. And because it manifests the beauty of Jesus, it glorifies God and has a power to change the world in a way that kingdom-of-the-world strategies never could.

BEING PRO-LIFE — KINGDOM STYLE

Here's an example. An unmarried eighteen-year-old woman, whom I'll call Becky, became pregnant.[8] She was afraid to tell her strict Christian parents because she was convinced they would disown her in disgrace and make her move out of the house. This in turn would jeopardize her plans to attend college and fulfill her dream of becoming a veterinarian. Consequently, she planned to have an abortion.

Becky confided in a friend of the family, whom I'll call Dorothy, a middle-aged, divorced woman who over the years had developed a special relationship with Becky. When Becky told Dorothy of her plan, Dorothy didn't give her a moralistic speech or perform a moral interrogation. She offered to help. If Becky chose to have an abortion, Dorothy offered to help her in the postabortion recovery. But, believing that it was in everyone's best interest to refrain from a violent solution and to rather go full term with this child, Dorothy lovingly encouraged Becky to think seriously about her planned course of action. Even more importantly, she offered to do whatever it took to make going full term feasible.

If Becky's parents kicked her out of the house (which they actually did), Dorothy offered her basement as a place to stay. It wasn't much, but it was something. Whatever financial and emotional support Becky needed throughout her pregnancy, Dorothy would provide as best as she was able. She ended up taking out a second mortgage on her house. If Becky wanted to give the baby up for adoption, Dorothy would help her with this. If Becky wanted to keep the child (which she ended up doing), Dorothy would help her with this as well. She became the godmother. And on top of this, Dorothy promised to work with Becky to help make it financially possible to pursue her dream of becoming a veterinarian. As a result, Becky went through with the pregnancy, moved in with Dorothy, and pursued her dream part-time, while both she and Dorothy raised her adorable daughter.

This, I believe, is an example of being pro-life *kingdom* style. Dorothy was willing to bleed to ascribe worth to Becky and her unborn child. It was her way of saying, "You and your baby are worth *this much* to me." Dorothy's decision wasn't rooted in any of the complex, ambiguous issues that pro-life and pro-choice groups argue over. She frankly didn't claim to know what the metaphysical status of the unborn child was at a given state in its development. Like most Americans, Dorothy had a sense that the use of the morning-after pill wasn't quite as tragic as partial-birth abortions or infant killing—but she couldn't articulate exactly why she felt this or say when the magic moment that made the fetus a full human person happened. But in terms of her relationship with Becky, this didn't matter. She only believed it is better to affirm life whenever possible rather than terminate it, and she was willing to communicate this conviction in any way she could—by paying a price.

The price Dorothy paid is much greater than the price of a vote, carrying a picket sign, or signing a petition. But this is why Dorothy's way of being pro-life is a distinctly kingdom way of being pro-life. It has nothing to do with her opinions about which limited, ambiguous, kingdom-of-the-world option is right, and it has everything to do with replicating Jesus' Calvary-quality love for others. It may be worth noting that, for a variety of complex reasons, Dorothy tended to vote pro-choice. Yet I would suggest that Dorothy was far more pro-life than many who profess to being pro-life on the grounds that they vote a certain way.

Dorothy's sacrifices not only allowed a child to be born and a young woman to be spared the emotional scars that usually accompany abortion; Dorothy's Calvary-quality action had a transforming effect on Becky, who felt a love she had unfortunately not experienced before. She experienced her worth as a person, despite her poor decisions. And whatever you think about abortion laws, the love Becky experienced from Dorothy had a power to transform her in a way that a law prohibiting her from having the abortion never could. It is the uniquely beautiful quality of "power under," and *that* is the power of the kingdom of God, the power that comes from bleeding for others. It is the power that looks like Calvary and that flows from Calvary.

The church is called to be a church of Dorothys, not just on the abortion issue, but on every issue. Rather than buying into and then fighting over the limited, divisive options of the kingdom of the world, we need to be the one tribe on the planet who thinks "outside the box." We need to be a peculiar people who live in the otherwise unasked question—what can we do to bleed as a means of manifesting *life*? While others posture and holler, we are to be a holy people who, knowing we are the worst of sinners, simply live in the question—how can we bleed for others? How can we sacrifice for and serve the gay, lesbian, and transgender community in a way that communicates to them their unsurpassable worth? How can we individually and collectively bleed in service to the homeless, the poor, and the racially oppressed? What does "power under" service look like to drug addicts, battered women, pregnant women, children in sexual bondage, and confused, needy people such as Janet Jackson?

The distinct kingdom question is not, How do you *vote*? The distinct kingdom question is, How do you *bleed*?

CHAPTER 8

ONE NATION under GOD?

Jesus refused to accept conventional wisdom.... His model of kingship,
and his vision of the kingdom of God, was not to "make the world safe for democracy"
by the exercise of sheer force, was not to effect a "balance of power" through
the threat of nuclear holocaust, was not to "rid the world of evil" through a never-ending
crusade of "war against terror." He would not rule by a sword, but by a towel.

LEE CAMP[1]

WE HAVE SEEN THAT THE MYTH OF THE CHRISTIAN NATION HARMS LOCAL
and global missions, influences us to trust "power over" rather than
"power under," and leads many Christians to the mistaken conclusion that their job is to protect and advance civil religion and morality rather than simply serve people. In this chapter I will discuss
a fifth negative consequence: it inclines kingdom people to view
America as a theocracy, like Old Testament Israel. As we will see,
this perspective damages the advancement of the kingdom of God.

First, consider the oft-cited, theocratic-sounding slogan that
America is "one nation under God" ...

THE PARADIGM OF ISRAEL

As a rallying slogan for our civil religion, the proclamation that we
are "one nation under God" arguably serves a useful social function,
for it gives many Americans a sense of shared values and vision. But
it is not a slogan kingdom people in America should take too seriously. We must always remember that, while some nations serve
law and order better than others, the powers that govern *all* nations
are to a significant extent corrupted by the polluting influence of
Satan. We should know that part of this influence is manifested

in a violent, nationalistic pride, often buttressed by a nationalistic religion. We are to live in such a way that we manifest the radical difference between the kingdom of God and every version of the kingdom of the world. Our job, in other words, is to manifest the *holiness* of the kingdom of God, and *that* is how we are to be a light of hope to the world.

When the theocratic-sounding slogan "one nation under God" is taken too seriously, it makes people think of America along the lines of Israel and the Old Testament rather than Jesus and the New Testament.[2] Just as God gave the Promised Land to Israel while vanquishing and enslaving opponents, so too, many believe, God gave America to white Europeans—while vanquishing all who resisted this takeover and enslaving others to build the nation. For obvious reasons, this baseless and racist theological interpretation of American history helps explain why the church remains the most segregated institution in America.

Just as God led Israel in the past, or so some believe, God leads America today. When America goes to war, therefore, God is on our side, just as he was on the side of Israel. For obvious reasons, this understanding does not endear this Christian warrior-God of America to all who are or have been the enemies of America or feel oppressed by America.

There are at least two conceptual problems with the Israel-theocratic paradigm, and two further negative consequences that result from it that we need to discuss. First, the conceptual problems.

IS AMERICA, OR WAS IT EVER, A THEOCRACY?

The first conceptual problem is that there is no reason to believe America ever was a theocracy. Unlike Israel, we have no biblical or empirical reason to believe God ever intended to be king over America in any unique sense. True, some of those who were part of the original European conquest of this continent claimed this, but why believe they were right?

Undoubtedly, part of the reason evangelicals accept this claim is the fact that fallen humans have always tended to fuse religious and nationalistic and tribal interests. We *want* to believe that God is on *our* side, supports *our* causes, protects *our* interests, and ensures *our* victories—which, in one form or another, is precisely what most of our nationalistic enemies also believe. So it has been for most people throughout history.

Related to this, fallen humans have a strong tendency to divinize our own values, especially those most dear to us. Feuerbach was at least partly correct: we tend to make God in our own image.[3] If something is important *to us*, we reason, then it must be important *to God*. Hence, we must in some sense be special to God for agreeing with him! Since political freedom is dear to American evangelicals, it seems obvious to them that it must also be dear to God. Indeed, it seems clear to many that God uniquely established America and leads America for the express purpose of promoting this supreme value around the globe.[4]

Now, we may (or may not) grant that it's "self-evident" that political freedom is the most precious thing a government can give its people. We may (or may not) think it would be good if every version of the kingdom of the world espoused this value. But on what basis can a follower of Jesus claim this is obviously a supreme value *for God?* Political freedom certainly wasn't a value emphasized by Jesus, for he never addressed the topic. He and various New Testament authors speak about freedom from sin, fear, and the Devil, but show no interest in political freedom.

In fact, until very recently, political freedom wasn't a value ever espoused by the church. To the contrary, most branches of the church *resisted* the idea that people can govern themselves when it first began to be espoused in the Enlightenment period. Yet now, quite suddenly, it's supposedly a preeminent *Christian* value—to the point of justifying the view that America is uniquely established and led by God because it emphasizes this value! And this many contemporary evangelicals regard as obvious!

This is an amazing and significant new twist on the Christian religion. Indeed, it arguably constitutes a *new nationalistic religion*—what we might call "the religion of American democracy." Like all religions, this religion has its own distinctive, theologized, revisionist history (for instance, the "manifest destiny" doctrine whereby God destined Europeans to conquer the land). It has its own distinctive message of salvation (political freedom), its own "set apart" people group (America and its allies), its own creed ("we hold these truths to be self-evident"), its own distinctive enemies (all who resist freedom and who are against America), its own distinctive symbol (the flag), and its own distinctive god (the national deity we are "under," who favors our causes and helps us win our battles).[5] This nationalistic religion co-opts Christian rhetoric, but it in fact has nothing to do with real Christianity, for it has nothing to do with the kingdom of God.

Not only is the supreme value of this new nationalistic religion (political freedom) not espoused in Scripture, as we've said, but the Calvary-quality love that *is* the supreme value espoused by the New Testament is impossible to live out consistently if one is also aligned with this nationalistic religion. Among other things, the nationalistic religion is founded on individual self-interest—the "right" to political freedom—whereas the kingdom of God is centered on self-sacrifice, replicating Calvary to all people at all times. Moreover, because it is a nationalistic religion, the religion of political freedom must use "power over" to protect and advance itself. As we have seen, however, the kingdom of God planted by and modeled by Jesus uses only "power under" to advance itself, and it does not protect itself by force. It is impossible to imitate Jesus, dying on the cross for those who crucified him, while at the same time killing people on the grounds that they are against political freedom. It is impossible to love your enemies and bless those who persecute you, while at the same time defending your right to political freedom by killing those who threaten you.

Now, I want to be clear: none of this detracts from the important kingdom-of-the-world value of political freedom. Nor is it meant to minimize the tremendous sacrifice many have made, and continue to make, to defend our freedom. It is only meant to highlight the fact that, however much one cherishes political freedom, a kingdom-of-God citizen must never elevate this to the status of a kingdom-of-God value. We must always preserve the holiness and beauty of the kingdom of God by not letting it get co-opted by a nationalistic religion—even, and especially, when we agree that the central value of the nationalistic religion is very important. We must never allow cultural sentiments to compromise our calling to be radically set apart from the masses by our willingness and capacity to love those nationalistic enemies that others despise.

The danger of kingdom people taking the slogan "one nation under God" too seriously is that we set ourselves up for idolatrous compromise. We may judge that God wants all people to be politically free. We may believe that to this extent God approves of America. But we have no grounds for thinking that America is for this reason a nation that is more "under God" than any other nation. As in all nations, God is working in America to further law and order as much as possible, and, as with all nations, America is under the strong corrupting influence of demonic powers. So while we may agree that the "one nation under God" slogan serves a useful civil function, as kingdom people we must never take it too seriously. The only people who can be meaningfully said to be "under God" in a kingdom-of-God way are those who are in fact manifesting the reign of God by mimicking Jesus' love expressed on Calvary (Eph. 5:1–2).

THE THEOCRATIC PROGRAM IS OVER

The second fundamental problem with viewing America as a theocracy is that God's theocratic program in the Old Testament was temporary, conditional—and ultimately abandoned. God formed Israel to be a distinct, set-apart, holy people in order to use them to reach the whole world. Through the descendants of Abraham, all the families of the world were to be blessed (Gen. 12:2–3). The

Israelites were to be God's ministers, his priests to the world. God took great pains (and inflicted great pains) to get this people into "the Promised Land" because it was strategic in accomplishing this global mission.

This nationalistic program, however, never worked well, and Israel eventually demanded an earthly king like other nations. Many of their leaders didn't listen to God and drove the country into ruin. Even more tragically, Israel forgot that its unique calling was not an end in itself. They were supposed to be set apart from the world so that they could effectively serve the world. But like so much of the church today, they became prideful of their unique holiness and judgmental of the people they were called to serve.

God, therefore, abandoned this nationalistic means of transforming the world. While God is by no means through with Israel, he is no longer using them or any other nation to grow his kingdom on the earth.[6] The kingdom is now growing through Jesus Christ who lives in and through his corporate body. In this sense, Jesus and the church constitute a new Israel.[7]

Unlike the nation of Israel, this new Israel, this new "royal priesthood" (1 Peter 2:9) is not to be conditioned by any nationalistic, ethnic, or ideological allegiances. To the contrary, it is to be comprised of people from every tribe, every tongue, and every nation (Rev. 5:9; 7:9; 21:24–26). Through his death and resurrection, Jesus utterly abolished all the typical kingdom-of-the-world categories that divide people: nation, race, gender, social and economic status, and so on. And inasmuch as the church is called to manifest everything Jesus died for, manifesting this divisionless "new humanity" (Eph. 2:14) lies at the heart of the kingdom commission.

In light of this, we must conclude that any suggestion that God has returned to his Old Testament theocratic mode of operation—as in raising up America as a uniquely favored nation—is not only unwarranted, it is a direct assault on the distinct holiness of Jesus Christ and the kingdom he died to establish. While one may or may not contend that America wields the sword more justly than most other versions of the kingdom of the world, under no circumstances is a kingdom-of-God participant justified in claiming that it is a nation that is more "under God" than any other nation in the world.

The holiness of the kingdom of God must be preserved. If Jesus refused to acknowledge and fight for Israel as God's favored nation—even though it was the one nation in history that actually held this status at one time—how much more must his followers refuse to acknowledge and fight for America as God's favored nation? To say it another way, if Jesus was committed solely to establishing a kingdom that had no intrinsic nationalistic or ethnic allegiances —not even with Israel—how much more should his followers be committed to expanding this unique, nonnationalistic kingdom?

OVERRELIANCE ON GOVERNMENT

We've discussed the two fundamental conceptual problems with "one nation under God." We turn now to two negative consequences this slogan has for the church.

First, people who believe America is in fact a "nation under God" may be inclined to view government as the handmaiden of God and thus inclined to rely on it to carry out the work God has called the church to carry out. More specifically, as with most other Americans, many Christians assume it's the church's job to take care of people's *spiritual* needs and the government's job to take care of people's *physical* needs. We preach the gospel while government is supposed to care for the poor, the homeless, the oppressed, the disabled, or the sick. Many would, in fact, deny they believe this, but based on how the church *acts*—which is always a far better indication of true belief than profession—the point is undeniable. The evangelical church as a whole is not known for its willingness to assume responsibility for these areas (though there *are* wonderful exceptions). And this, I submit, is largely due to the fact that we trust government to carry out these duties.

Now, it is certainly good for governments to take care of people's physical needs as much as it is able to (by taxing citizens, rightly prioritizing the budget, and so forth). But it's not a good thing for Christians to *rely* on government to carry out this function and thus limit themselves to ministering to people's spiritual needs. As William Booth (founder of the Salvation Army) saw so clearly a century and a half ago, it's the church's job to minister to *people*, not just their spiritual needs. Indeed, there's no biblical warrant for separating a person's physical needs from their spiritual ones. When a person is without food, without shelter, and without hope, this is a physical *and* spiritual issue. Hence, rather than relying on government, the church is to take responsibility to do all it can to care for people in every possible way.

What would happen if, instead of waiting on Uncle Sam to solve social issues, the church took responsibility? What would happen if kingdom people honored Jesus' command not to own anything (Luke 14:33) and followed the kingdom principle of giving to those in need and taking in those who are without a home (Luke 6:30–31, 35–36; 10:29–37; Rom. 12:13; Eph. 4:28)? What would happen if wealthy suburban congregations took it upon themselves to build affordable housing for the poor? What if we actually took seriously Jesus' teaching that we are to treat everyone in need as though they were Jesus himself (Matt. 25:34–46)?

Such kingdom work would obviously require tremendous sacrifice on our part. Many of us would have to readjust our lifestyles to fund such ministries. Perhaps this in part explains why we so often overlook it and rather choose to spend our time tweaking the civil religion and concerning ourselves merely with the "spiritual" needs of people. But precisely because it requires us to bleed, this sort of sacrificial activity is a distinctly kingdom one. It is the essence of what we are called to do.

While it is good for government to be compassionate, of course, kingdom people need to remember that the hope of the world doesn't lie in government; it lies in Jesus Christ and in the willingness of his people to mimic his example (Eph. 5:1–2). We are not to rely on government to do what God has called us to do: namely, serve people by sacrificing our own time, energy, and resources.

Only insofar as we do this are we the authentic body of Christ manifesting the holy kingdom of God.

If the church understood itself to be a tribe of kingdom soldiers stationed in enemy-occupied territory, whose sole mission was to advance the cause of their King by imitating what he did for them on the cross, we would rely on the government much less and take responsibility to serve the needs of people much more. Unfortunately, the "one nation under God" mindset has contributed to the loss of this spiritual warfare mindset, and thus the shirking of much of the American church's responsibility in service to our nation and to the world.

AN UNWARRANTED MODEL OF EVANGELISM

Closely related to this is a second negative consequence of taking "one nation under God" too seriously. As noted above, this nationalistic slogan influences many Christians to turn to the Old Testament more than the New in their understanding of America and of the role of the church within America. Consequently, Christians often turn to the models of Old Testament "watchmen" (as in Ezek. 33) and of John the Baptist to understand what they are supposed to be doing in the culture, rather than to the model of Jesus. Instead of living to sacrifice for others, we become the official "sin-pointer-outers." Instead of gaining a reputation of being humble servants who manifest Calvary-quality love, we gain a reputation for being moralistic and self-righteous. And predictably, we drive away the tax collectors and prostitutes of our day, just as the Pharisees did, rather than attracting them, as Jesus did.

The error of this thinking is obvious once we understand that God's nationalistic agenda ended with Christ. Though it never truly functioned in this manner, Israel was intended to be a theocracy. The Israelites understood themselves to be in a covenant relationship with God, and they also understood that the job of watchmen and prophets such as John the Baptist was to hold the people and their leaders accountable to this covenant. As a matter

of principle, prophets and watchmen didn't hold non-Jews accountable to God's unique covenant with Israel; their role was only to
hold Jews accountable, for the covenant that formed the basis of
this accountability was made only with the Jews.

This is why John the Baptist pointed out the sin of Herod—a
Jewish governor—but not the sin of Pilate or any other Gentile
leader (Matt. 14:3–4). That's why Nathan exposed the sin of David
(2 Sam. 12:1–12), but not the sins of any pagan kings, even though
their sins were, by Israeli covenantal standards, often worse. And
that's also why Jesus, assuming the role of a prophet, exposed the
hypocrisy of the Jewish religious leaders, but never concerned himself with Gentile religious or political leaders.

While there is a comparable role for prophets and watchmen
within intimate Christian communities, these roles have no appli-
cation to Christians within American society as a whole. God's
nationalistic program came to an end with the death and resurrection of Jesus, and in any case, his covenant with Israel was not a
covenant with America or any other nation. What's more, the self-
understanding of most people in America today is worlds removed
from the self-understanding of Jews under the Old Covenant.
When Christians model themselves after Old Covenant prophets
and watchmen, they end up trying to hold people accountable to
things these people know little about and care even less about. It
is at best ineffective, and at worst it is positively harmful to the
advancement of the kingdom of God.

To illustrate, one of the most clear expressions of the Old Testament model of evangelism today is found in an increasingly popular
form of witnessing sometimes called "confrontational evangelism."[8]
In this model people are taught that it is the job of Christians to
get others to realize they have broken one or more of the Ten Commandments and that they, therefore, deserve God's eternal wrath.
The goal is to get people to see their need for a Savior.

The trouble with this approach, of course, is that despite the
veneer of civil religion, most people in America aren't worried
about whether they break one of the Ten Commandments now and

then, and they certainly don't see the logic behind the claim that infractions of this sort warrant everlasting damnation. Just because the evangelist thinks this doesn't mean the person they're confronting thinks this, and the lack of shared presuppositions makes the encounter odd at best. The situation is no different from, say, a Muslim telling a non-Muslim stranger who happens to be eating pork that he deserves to go to hell because the Koran forbids eating pork. Why should the non-Muslim care what the Koran says?

The people that Old Testament prophets and watchmen held accountable were those who could be expected to accept the terms of accountability. As Jews, they knew they were supposed to obey the revealed law and knew that the job of prophets and watchmen was to help them do this. But this is precisely what is missing in America—and precisely what the "one nation under God" mindset causes some to overlook. When Christians confront people on the basis of presuppositions not shared by the people they confront, they come across as rude (hence unloving, 1 Cor. 13:4–5) and usually render the gospel less credible to the people they confront.[9] What is not generally communicated to the people being evangelized is the one thing we are called to communicate: namely, sacrificial, Calvary-quality love modeled after Jesus.

PAUL'S MODEL OF NON-JEWISH EVANGELISM

It's significant to note that while Paul preached from the Jewish Scriptures when evangelizing Jews (as in Acts 17:2), he did not appeal to the Old Testament when evangelizing Gentiles. Rather than making his case on what he, as a Jew, believed, he made his case on the basis of what his Gentile audience believed.

The clearest example of this approach is found in Acts 17. While discussing Christ "in the marketplace," Paul encountered some Stoic and Epicurean philosophers who took him to the Areopagus to share his views with fellow philosophers (v. 19). Paul began his speech not by "confronting their sin," but by commending them for being "extremely religious." Remarkably, he based his commendation on the fact that these folks had so many idolatrous objects of worship (vv. 22–23)! Now, had these philosophers been Jewish, Paul's approach may have been quite different, for Jews of this time were expected to know and honor the Old Testament's prohibition on idols. But these were Gentiles, so holding them accountable for things they didn't themselves believe would have been unwise, arrogant, and rude. Though their idols deeply offended Paul as a Jew (v. 16), he complimented them for their sincerity. This was a loving approach to take, for love believes the best, looks for the best, and hopes for the best in everyone (1 Cor. 13:7).

Paul then noted that one of their "objects of ... worship" contained an inscription, "To an unknown god." This acknowledged ignorance on the part of the philosophers provided Paul with an opening to present the gospel. "What ... you worship as unknown," Paul said, "this I proclaim to you" (v. 23). This too was a Christlike, loving approach. Rather than shooting at what one believes is wrong in another's life or way of thinking, love looks for the best, looks for truth, and then builds on it. A loving approach to evangelism finds an area of expressed need, uncertainty, or longing and then seeks to meet it as Christ would.

What is amazing, however, is that when Paul presents the gospel to these people, he doesn't do so on the basis of Scripture as he did earlier with Jews (vv. 1–2). Rather, he quotes pagan philosophers (v. 28), for these are the sources that have credibility to these folks, not Scripture. Paul builds his case on truths he finds in what the Epicureans and Stoics already believe. He presents Christ as the fulfillment of their own beliefs and the goal of the innate longing God has placed in all people at all times (vv. 26–27). While some "scoffed" at his claims, others were intrigued enough to want to consider it further (v. 32).

When evangelizing people who do not share one's own presuppositions, this is the loving and wise approach to take. Unfortunately, Christians who take the "one nation under God" mindset too seriously are lulled into thinking that Americans generally share kingdom presuppositions. Being duped by the quasi-Christian civil religion, they treat average American citizens almost as if they were Christians who simply weren't living up to their calling. They thus think they're doing people a favor by holding them accountable to things that are, in fact, foreign to them. As we've said, the result is that they come across as odd, arrogant, and rude, rather than loving.

Instead of respecting the integrity of people's beliefs, building on what is true about them, we simply point out what we think is wrong. Rather than looking for the best, believing the best, and hoping for the best, we zero in on what we believe is the worst. Rather than serving people by taking the time to understand their worldview from the inside and looking for an opening within this worldview, we assume they think like us and speak to them from within our own worldview. Consequently, we unwittingly undermine the credibility of the gospel and do not communicate the central thing we are called to communicate—Calvary-quality love.

Our approach will be more like Paul's if we can wake up and see the radical disparity between the civil religion of America— expressed in the "one nation under God" slogan—and the authentic kingdom of God. People who are merely shaped by the civil religion of America are no closer to the kingdom of God than people shaped by the civil religion of Buddhism, Islam, or Hinduism. It's nothing more than the civil religious veneer of the culture. When we understand this, we see that our job is to serve our fellow Americans by building bridges that connect us with them and entering into their unique worldview, just as we would if we were in, say, Indonesia, Tanzania, Bangladesh, or any other "non-Christian" country—and just as Paul did with his Gentile audience.

CHAPTER 9

CHRISTIANS AND VIOLENCE: CONFRONTING THE TOUGH QUESTIONS

Jesus said to him, "Put your sword back into its place;
for all who take the sword will perish by the sword."
MATTHEW 26:52

Throughout this book I've attempted to help kingdom people wake up to the radical difference between the kingdom of the sword and the kingdom of the cross as a means of motivating us to live out the unique call of God's kingdom more authentically and more consistently. To accomplish this, I've admittedly painted with broad, contrasting strokes. If we resolve that the kingdom always looks like Jesus, and if we therefore commit to living in love as Christ loves us on a moment-by-moment basis, it will usually be clear what a kingdom individual or community should do in a particular situation—usually, but not always. For in the ambiguous war zone in which we live, the lines between exercising "power over" and "power under" are sometimes fuzzy, giving rise to an assortment of ethical questions. Not only this, but it is not always clear how our absolute allegiance to the "power under" kingdom affects our participation in the "power over" kingdom.

Now, the particular way we might answer these sorts of questions is less important than whether or not we approach such questions in a distinctly kingdom fashion. We will always have to wrestle with ambiguity in this life. The ultimate question is, do we wrestle with this ambiguity from a distinctly kingdom-of-God perspective, or do we allow ourselves to be pulled into a kingdom-of-the-world perspective as we seek to answer them? The goal of this book has not been to provide the "right" answer to ambiguous ethical questions but to help kingdom people appreciate the urgency of preserving the unique kingdom-of-God perspective on all questions and on life as a whole.

Still, I believe it may be helpful to some readers to address a few of these difficult issues. What follows is my own wrestling with five of the questions I have most frequently been asked whenever I've publicly presented the perspective articulated in this book.

1. WHAT ABOUT SELF-DEFENSE?

You argue that a central aspect of the kingdom of God is the refusal to return evil with evil by using violence. Are you saying that if an enemy threatened to kill you, your wife, or your children, you wouldn't use violence to protect yourself or them?

The New Testament commands us never to "repay anyone evil for evil," but instead to "overcome evil with good" (Rom. 12:17, 21; cf. 1 Thess. 5:15; 1 Peter 3:9). Jesus said, "Do not resist an evildoer. But if anyone strikes you on the right cheek, turn the other also" (Matt. 5:39). He also said, "Love your enemies, do good to those who hate you, bless those who curse you, pray for those who abuse you" (Luke 6:27–28). The teaching seems pretty straightforward, yet this very straightforwardness presents us with a dilemma.

On the one hand, we who confess Jesus as Lord don't want to say that Jesus and other New Testament authors are simply off their rockers in telling us not to resist evildoers, to repay evil with good, to love our enemies, and to pray for and bless people who mistreat us. If our confession of faith means anything, it means we have to take this teaching seriously. On the other hand, we have to admit that it's hard to take this teaching seriously when it comes to extreme situations such as having to protect ourselves and our family from an intruder. Not only would most of us resist an evildoer in this situation, killing him if necessary, but most of us would see it as immoral if we *didn't* use violence to resist such an evildoer. How can refusing to protect your family by any means be considered moral? Isn't it more loving, and thus more ethical, to protect your family at all costs?

How do we resolve this dilemma? It helps somewhat to remember that the word Jesus uses for "resist" (*antistenai*) doesn't imply passively allowing something to take place. It rather connotes resisting a forceful action with a similar forceful action.[1] Jesus is thus forbidding responding to violent action with *similar* violent action. He's teaching us not to take on the violence of the one who is acting violently toward us. He's teaching us to respond to evil in a way that is consistent with loving them. But he's not by any means saying *do nothing*. As Wink notes, "Jesus ... abhors both passivity and violence."[2]

Still, the teaching is problematic, for most of us would instinctively use violence, and feel justified using it, to protect our family from an intruder.

The most common way people resolve this dilemma is by convincing themselves that the "enemies" Jesus was referring to are not *our* enemies—for example, people who attack our family (or our nation, our standard of living, and so on). Jesus must have been referring to "other kinds" of enemies, less serious enemies, or something of the sort. We tell ourselves that when violence is justified —as in "just war" ethics—Jesus' teachings do not apply.[3] This approach allows us to feel justified, if not positively "Christian," killing intruders and bombing people who threaten our nation—so long as we are nice to our occasionally grumpy neighbors. Unfortunately, this common-sensical interpretation makes complete nonsense of Jesus' teaching.

The whole point of Jesus' teaching is to tell disciples that their attitude toward "enemies" should be *radically different*. "If you do good to those who do good to you," Jesus added, "what credit is that to you? For even sinners do the same" (Luke 6:33). Everybody instinctively hates those who hate them and believes they are justified killing people who might kill them or their loved ones. Jesus is saying, "Be radically different." This is why Jesus (and Paul) didn't qualify the "enemies" or "evildoers" he taught us to love and not violently oppose. Jesus didn't say, "Love your enemies until they threaten you, until it seems justified to resort to violence, or until it seems impractical to do so." Enemies are enemies precisely *because* they threaten us on some level, and it *always* seems justified and practically expedient to resist them, if not harm them when necessary. Jesus simply said, "Love your enemies" and "Don't resist evildoers." Note that some of the people he was speaking to would before long confront "enemies" who would feed them and their families to lions for amusement.

The teaching could not be more radical, and as kingdom people we have to take it seriously. At the same time, what do we do with the fact that most of us know we would not take it seriously, let alone obey it, in extreme situations such as our family coming under attack?

As with all of Jesus' teachings, it's important to place this teaching in the broader context of Jesus' kingdom ministry. Jesus' teachings aren't a set of pacifistic laws people are to merely obey, however unnatural and immoral they seem. Rather, his teachings are descriptions of what life in God's domain looks like and prescriptions for how we are to cultivate this alternative form of life. In other words, Jesus' isn't saying, "As much as you want to resist an evildoer and kill your enemy, and as unnatural and immoral as it seems, *act* loving toward him." He's rather saying, "Cultivate the kind of life where loving your enemy becomes natural for you." He's not merely saying, "*Act* different from others"; he's saying, "*Be* different from others." This is simply what it means to cultivate a life that looks like Jesus, dying on a cross for the people who crucified him.

How does this insight help address our dilemma? A person who lives with the "normal" tit-for-tat kingdom-of-the-world mindset would instinctively resort to violence to protect himself and his family. Loving his attacker and doing good to them would be the furthest thing from his mind. As with the Jerusalem that Jesus wept over, the "things that make for peace" would be "hidden from

[his] eyes" (Luke 19:41–42). Indeed, from this kingdom-of-the-world perspective, Jesus' teaching seems positively absurd.

But how might a person who cultivated a nonviolent, kingdom-of-God mindset and lifestyle on a daily basis respond differently to an attacker? How might a person who consistently *lived* in Christlike love (Eph. 5:1–2) operate in this situation?

For one thing, such a person would have cultivated a kind of character and wisdom that wouldn't automatically default to self-protective violence. Because he would genuinely love his enemy, he would have the desire to look for, and the wisdom to see, any nonviolent alternative to stopping his family's attacker if one was available. He would *want* to do good to his attacker. This wouldn't be a matter of him trying to obey an irrational rule to "look for an alternative in extreme situations," for in extreme situations no one is thinking about obeying rules! Rather, it would be in the Christlike nature of this person to see nonviolent alternatives if they were present. This person's moment-by-moment discipleship in love would have given him a Christlike wisdom that a person whose mind was conformed to the pattern of the tit-for-tat world would not have (Rom. 12:2). Perhaps they'd see that pleading with, startling, or distracting the attacker would be enough to save themselves and their family. Perhaps they'd discern a way to allow their family to escape harm by placing themselves in harm's way.

Not only this, but this person's day-by-day surrender to God would have cultivated a sensitivity to God's Spirit that would enable him to discern God's leading in the moment, something the "normal" kingdom-of-the-world person would be oblivious to. This Christlike person might be divinely led to say something or do something that would disarm the attacker emotionally, spiritually, or even physically.

For example, I heard of a case in which a godly woman was about to be sexually assaulted. Just as she was being pinned to the ground with a knife to her throat, out of nowhere she said to her attacker, "Your mother forgives you." She had no conscious idea where the statement came from. What she didn't know was that her attacker's violent aggression toward women was rooted in a heinous thing he had done as a teenager to his now deceased mother. The statement shocked the man and quickly reduced him to a sobbing little boy.

The woman seized the opportunity to make an escape and call the police who quickly apprehended the man in the park where the attack took place. He was still there, sobbing. The man later credited the woman's inspired statement with being instrumental in him eventually turning his life over to Christ. The point is that, in any given situation, God may see possibilities for nonviolent solutions that we cannot see, and a person who has learned to "live by the Spirit" is open to being led by God in these directions (Gal. 5:16, 18).

Not only this, but a person who has cultivated a kingdom-of-God outlook on life would have developed the capacity to assess this situation from an eternal perspective. Having made Jesus her example on a moment-by-moment basis, she would know—not just as a rule, but as a heartfelt reality—the truth that living in love is more important than life itself. Her values would not be exhaustively defined by temporal expediency. Moreover, she would have cultivated a trust in God that would free her from defining winning and losing in terms of temporal outcomes. She would have confidence in the resurrection. As such, she would be free from the "preserve my interests at all costs" mindset of the world.

Of course it's possible that, despite a person's loving wisdom and openness to God, a man whose family was attacked might see no way to save himself and his family except to harm the attacker or even to take his life. What would such a person do in this case? I think it is clear from Jesus' teachings, life, and especially his death that *Jesus* would choose nonviolence. So, it seems to me that a person who was totally conformed to the image of Jesus Christ, who had thoroughly cultivated a kingdom mind and heart, would do the same.

At the same time, I have to confess that I'm not sure this is what *I'd* do. I honestly admit that, like most people, I don't yet quite see how it would be moral to do what I believe Jesus would do. Yet I have to assume that my disagreement with Jesus is due to my not having sufficiently cultivated a kingdom heart and mind. If I felt I had to harm or take the life of another to prevent what clearly seemed to be a greater evil, I could not feel righteous or even justified about it. Like Bonhoeffer who, despite his pacifism, plotted to assassinate Hitler, I could only plead for God's mercy.

What we must never do, however, is acquiesce to our worldly condition by rationalizing away Jesus' clear kingdom prescriptions. We must rather strive every moment of our life to cultivate the kind of mind and heart that increasingly sees the rightness and beauty of Jesus' teachings and thus would naturally respond to an extreme, threatening situation in a loving, nonviolent manner.

2. WHAT ABOUT CHRISTIANS IN THE MILITARY?

Do you think Jesus' teaching about not resisting evildoers implies that Christians should never serve in the military?

Some soldiers responded to the preaching of John the Baptist by asking him what they should do. John gave them some ethical instruction, but interestingly enough, he didn't tell them to leave the army (Luke 3:14). Likewise, Jesus praised the faith of a centurion and healed his servant while not saying a word about the centurion's occupation (Matt. 8:5–13; Luke 7:1–10). Another centurion acknowledged Christ as the Son of God at the cross (Mark 15:39) without any negative comment being made about his military involvement. And the first Gentile to receive the good news of the gospel was a centurion described as a God-fearing man (Acts 10:22, 34–35). Clearly none of these texts endorse military involvement. But just as clearly, neither do they condemn it. For these and other reasons, most American Christians accept that the New Testament does not forbid serving in the military.

While I respect that people will have differing convictions about this, I must confess that I find it impossible to reconcile Jesus' teaching (and the teaching of the whole New Testament) concerning our call to love our enemies and never return evil with evil with the choice to serve (or not resist being drafted) in the armed forces in a capacity that might require killing someone.[4] The texts cited above show that the gospel can reach people who serve in the military. They also reveal that John the Baptist, Jesus, and the earliest Christians gave military personnel "space," as it were, to work out the implications of their faith vis-à-vis their service. But I don't see that they warrant making military service, as a matter of principle, an exception to the New Testament's teaching that kingdom people are to never return evil with evil.

The traditional response to the tension between the New Testament's uniform teaching, on the one hand, and taking up arms to defend one's country, on the other, is to argue that fighting in the military is permissible if one's military is fighting a "just war." As time-honored as this traditional position is, I'm not at all convinced it is adequate.[5]

For one thing, why should kingdom people assume that considerations of whether violence is justified or not have any relevance to whether a kingdom person engages in violence? Jesus is our Lord, not a human-constructed notion of justice. And neither Jesus nor any other New Testament author ever qualified their prohibitions on the use of violence. As George Zabelka remarked, the "just war" theory is "something that Christ never taught or even hinted at."[6] Indeed, as we saw above, Jesus goes out of his way to stress that his radical teaching on loving enemies sets his disciples apart precisely because it is *not* common-sensical (Luke 6:32). His disciples aren't to love and bless those who persecute them when it makes sense to do so and to fight back and perhaps kill them when it makes sense to do so (that is, when it's "just")—for, as a matter of fact, it *never* makes sense to love and bless a persecutor, and it *always* makes sense to fight back and kill them if you have to!

No, however much we might wish it were otherwise, there is no plausible way to insert a "just war" exception clause into Jesus' teachings. We are not to resist evildoers or return evil with evil— period. We are to love our enemies, turn the other cheek, bless those who persecute us, pray for people who mistreat us, and return evil with good—period.

Now, many have argued that they found grounds for a "just war" exception to Jesus' teachings in Romans 13. Since Paul in this passage grants that the authority of government ultimately comes from God and that God uses it to punish wrongdoers (Rom. 13:1–5), it seems permissible for Christians to participate in this violent activity, they argue, at least when the Christian is sure it is "just." Unfortunately, this argument is strained in several ways.

First, while Paul encourages Christians to be *subject to* whatever sword-wielding authorities they find themselves under, nothing in this passage suggests the Christians should *participate in* the government's sword-wielding activity. Second, as John Yoder has noted, Romans 13 must be read as a continuation of Romans 12, in which Paul tells disciples to (among other things) "bless those who persecute you" (v. 14); "do not repay anyone evil for evil" (v. 17); and especially, "never avenge yourselves, but leave room for the wrath of God; for it is written, 'Vengeance is mine, I will repay, says the Lord'" (v. 19). Leaving vengeance to God, we are to instead feed our enemies when they are hungry and give them water when they are thirsty (v. 20). Instead of being "overcome by evil," we are to "overcome evil with good" (v. 21).

In the next several verses, Paul specifies that sword-wielding authorities are one means by which God executes vengeance (13:4). Since this is the very same vengeance disciples were just *forbidden* to exercise (12:19, *ekdikeo*) it seems to follow, as Yoder argues, that the "vengeance" that is recognized as being within providential control when exercised by government is the same "vengeance" that Christians are told *not* to exercise."[7] In other words, we may acknowledge that in certain circumstances authorities carry out a good function in wielding the sword against wrongdoers, but that doesn't mean people who are committed to following Jesus should *participate* in it. Rather, it seems we are to leave such matters to God who uses sword-wielding authorities to carry out his will in society.

Thirdly, even if one were to concede, for the sake of argument, that a follower of Jesus may participate in violence if it is "just," we have to wonder how a kingdom person could confidently determine whether or not any particular war is in fact "just." Few wars have been fought in which both sides didn't believe their violence against the other side was justified. The reality is that the criteria one uses to determine what is and is not "just" is largely a function of where one is born and how one is raised. How much confidence should a kingdom-of-God citizen place in *that*?

For example, unlike most other groups throughout history and even today, modern Americans tend to view personal and political freedom as an important criteria to help determine whether a war is "just." We kill and die for our freedom and the freedom of others. But why should a kingdom person think killing for this reason is a legitimate exception to the New Testament's command to love and bless enemies? Can they be certain *God* holds this opinion?

Of course it seems perfectly obvious to most Americans that killing to defend and promote freedom is justified, but fundamental aspects of one's culture always seem obvious to people embedded in the culture. This criterion of personal freedom certainly hasn't been obvious to most people throughout history, including most Christians throughout history. And it's "obviously" *wrong* to many non-Americans—including many Christians—around the globe today. Even more importantly, it certainly isn't obvious in the teachings of Jesus or the whole of Scripture. In this light, kingdom people in all countries need to seriously examine the extent to which the ideal that leads them to think a war is or is not "just" is the result of their own cultural conditioning.

Assessing this is no easy matter. It helps to be mindful that the person you may end up killing in war probably believes, as strongly as you, that they are also fighting for a "just" cause. It also helps to consider the possibility that they are disciples of Jesus just like you, perhaps even mistakenly thinking their cause is a function of their discipleship just as some American soldiers believe. You have to believe that all of *their* thinking is merely the result of their cultural conditioning—for you obviously believe *they're* wrong to the point of being willing to kill them—while also being convinced that *your own* thinking is *not* the result of cultural conditioning. Can you be absolutely sure of this? Your fidelity to the kingdom of God, your life, and the lives of others are all on the line.

But suppose, for the sake of argument, we grant not only that justified violence provides an exception to Jesus' teaching but also that political freedom (or any other particular ideal) *is* a legitimate criteria for determining if violence is justified. This doesn't by any means yet settle the matter for a kingdom person contemplating enlisting in war (or not resisting being drafted into war). For one has to further appreciate that there are many *other* variables alongside the central criterion of justice that affect whether a particular war is in fact "just."

Do you know—*can* you know—the myriad of personal, social, political, and historical factors that have led to any particular conflict and that bear upon whether or not it is "justified"? For example, do you truly understand all the reasons your enemy gives for going to war against your nation, and are you certain they are altogether illegitimate? Are you certain your government has sought out all possible nonviolent means of resolving the conflict before deciding to take up arms? Are you certain the information you've been given about a war is complete, accurate, and objective? Do you know the *real* motivation of the leaders who will be commanding you to kill or be killed for "the cause," as opposed to the propaganda those leaders put out? Are you certain that the ultimate motivation isn't financial or political gain for certain people in high places? Are you certain that the war isn't in part motivated by personal grievances or done simply to support or advance the already extravagant lifestyle of most Americans? Given what we know about the corrupting influence of demonic powers in all nations, and given what we know about how the American government (like all other governments) has at times misled the public about what was really going on in the past (e.g., the Vietnam War), these questions must be wrestled with seriously.[8] Fidelity to the kingdom, your life, and the lives of others are at stake.

Yet even these questions do not resolve the issue for a kingdom person, who must know not only that a war is justified but that each and every particular battle they fight, and each and every life they may snuff out, is justified. However justified a war may be, commanders often make poor decisions about particular battles they engage in that are not just and that gratuitously waste innocent lives. While militaries sometimes take actions against officers who have their troops engage in unnecessary violence, the possibility (and even inevitability) of such unjust activity is typically considered "acceptable risk" so long as the overall war is just. But on what grounds should a person who places loyalty to Jesus over their commander accept this reasoning?

The fact that a war is justified means nothing to the innocent lives that are wasted, and the question is, how can a kingdom person be certain in *each* instance that they are not participating in the unnecessary and unjust shedding of innocent blood? It's questionable enough that a follower of Jesus would kill their national enemy rather than bless them simply because it's in the interest of their nation for them to do so. But what are we to think of the possibility that a follower of Jesus would kill someone who is not an enemy simply because someone higher in rank told them to?

The tragic reality is that most people contemplating entering the armed forces (or contemplating not refusing their draft), whether they be American or, say, Iraqi, North Korean, or Chinese, don't seriously ask these sorts of questions. Out of their cultural conditioning, most blindly *assume* their authorities are trustworthy, that their cause is justified, and that each person they are told to kill is a justified killing.[9] They unquestioningly believe the propaganda and obey the commands they're given. Throughout history, soldiers have, for the most part, been the unquestioning pawns of ambitious, egotistical rulers and obedient executors of their superior's commands. They were hired assassins who killed because someone told them to and their cultural conditioning made it "obvious" to them that it was a good and noble thing to do. So it has been for ages, and so it will be so long as the people and nations operate out of their self-interest.

But there is an alternative to this ceaseless, bloody merry-go-round: it is the kingdom of God. To belong to this kingdom is to crucify the fleshly desire to live out of self-interest and tribal interest, and to thus crucify the fallen impulse to protect these interests through violence. To belong to this revolutionary kingdom is to purge your heart of "all bitterness and wrath and anger and wrangling and slander, together with all malice" (Eph. 4:31)—however "justified" and understandable these sentiments might be. To belong to this counterkingdom is to "live in love, as Christ loved us and gave himself up for us" (Eph. 5:2). It is to live the life of Jesus Christ, the life that manifests the truth that it is better to serve than to be served and better to die than to kill. It is, therefore, to opt out of the kingdom-of-the-world war machine and manifest a radically different, beautiful, loving way of life. To refuse to kill for patriotic reasons is to show "we actually take our identity in Christ more seriously than our identity with the empire, the nation-state, or the ethnic terror cell whence we come," as Lee Camp says.[10]

So, while I respect the sincerity and courage of Christians who may disagree and feel it their duty to defend their country with violence, I honestly see no way to condone a Christian's decision to kill on behalf of any country—or for any other reason.

3. HAVEN'T SOME WARS RESULTED IN GOOD THINGS?

Though it was brutally violent, wasn't the Civil War a good thing in-as-much as it freed blacks in this country? As costly as it was, wasn't it a good thing that thousands of American and British soldiers were willing to kill and be killed to resist the advancement of the Third Reich? If Christians would have "turned the other cheek" and "loved their enemies" in these situations, blacks would still be enslaved, the Jews possibly exterminated, and much of the world possibly under Nazi rule.

It was obviously a good thing that blacks were freed from slavery and that the Third Reich was stopped. Other wars have produced positive outcomes, despite their carnage. For people who think only in terms of the kingdom of the world, this settles the matter: the good goal justifies the bloody means. From a kingdom-of-God perspective, however, the matter cannot be settled so quickly. Four further things must be said.

First, a kingdom person can agree that the outcome of a war was to some degree good without saying that the war itself was a Christian war or that it was good that Christians fought in it. As we have noted throughout this book, for the sake of the holiness of the kingdom, we must guard against labeling *Christian* everything that might be considered comparatively good. The kingdom of God is not merely the goodness of the kingdom of the world. Rather, the kingdom of God is the radical *alternative* to the kingdom of world. It is not merely good: *it is beautiful.* And there's nothing beautiful about war, however good its outcome may be.

Second, it's not the case that if all who profess Christ had "turned the other cheek" and "loved their enemies" blacks would still be enslaved and the world would now be under Nazi rule. To the contrary, it was mostly nominal Christians who enslaved blacks and who supported the Nazis! Had professing Christians been remotely like Jesus in the first place, there would have been no slavery or war for us to wonder about what *would have happened* had Christians loved their enemies and turned the other cheek![11]

There's a general principle behind this observation: the thing that creates the need for violence is the thing that ensures it will be countered with more violence—namely, the idolatrous depravity of the human heart. So long as hearts are depraved, people will live and die by the sword, for the tit-for-tat kingdom is forever exchanging blows. There is therefore no need to worry about the theoretical possibility of too many people "turning the other cheek" and "loving their enemies." Until God's kingdom is established on the earth, we can unfortunately be assured there will always be governments and others creating situations that call for violence, and governments and others willing to address that situation through violent means.

This leads to our third point. The kingdom person must always remember that God is the Lord of all creation and Lord over all the nations. As Lord of all, God takes responsibility for the governance of the world. Though all versions of the kingdom of the world are polluted by the influence of the fallen powers, God is the one who ultimately gives them their "power over" authority, who sets the general parameters of the amount of good and evil they can accomplish, and who thus takes responsibility for the care of the world as a whole. He is the one who takes responsibility to orchestrate the sword-wielding powers he finds in the world (Rom. 13:2–4).

Though much takes place through these authorities that is against God's will, kingdom people must trust God's ability to wisely manage the whole. We are not to "worry about our life," let alone the life of the world (Matt. 6:25). God uses the power of the sword to keep law and order, and though agents can and do use this power for evil, God ensures overall law and order will be maintained in the long run. Indeed, if need be, he can use the evil of one nation to keep the evil of another nation in check. Hence, no evil scheme of any person or any nation can thwart his ultimate purposes for creation (e.g., Job 42:2; Ps. 47:2–3, 7–8; 66:7; 75:6–7; Isa. 40:22–23). He is the God of all gods, the Lord of all lords, and the King of all kings (e.g., Deut. 10:17; Ps. 136:3; 1 Tim. 6:15; Rev. 19:16).

This means that kingdom people must leave to God the ultimate responsibility of governing the world and instead focus their attention on living out the radically distinctive call of the kingdom. We must not allow our fallen and fallible ideas about "what the world needs" to compromise the unique call on our life to live in Christlike love, even toward our nationalistic enemies. We must never let expediency replace faithfulness as the motivation of our behavior. Though it may violate our fallen "common sense" to do so, we must remember that Christ's death on the cross wasn't "commonsensical." To the contrary, Paul admits it is "foolishness" (1 Cor. 1:18, 23). Jesus didn't concern himself with fixing or steering the Roman government. He entrusted this matter to his Father and allowed himself to be crucified by the Roman government.

Of course, from a kingdom-of-the-world perspective, our refusal to operate according to common sense—that is, opting out of the "save the world through violence" mindset—will undoubtedly seem irresponsible. "It's your duty as a citizen of your nation to defend it—lest evil take over," we may hear. This has been the bloody mantra of all versions of the kingdom of the world throughout history. While we should worry about being despised because we're viewed as self-righteous hypocrites (see chap. 7), we should never worry about being despised because we refuse to participate in a culture of violence (Luke 6:22; John 15:20). Our response can only be to testify that we have a higher duty to a greater king and a greater country—and to invite our antagonists to join us in fulfilling this higher duty and serving this greater country.

Finally, not only are kingdom people called to trust God's ultimate lordship over the nations as we walk in humble obedience to Christ, we are also to trust that he will use our sacrificial obedience to Christ to accomplish his purposes in the world. It is the power of the cross, not the power of the sword, that holds the hope of the world, for the power of the cross is also the power of the resurrection. Even if it looks like evil gains the upper hand as we return evil with kindness rather than retaliate with violence, we are to know by faith that this apparent loss is only apparent.

We must remember that for three days it certainly looked like the Devil had won, but Christ's resurrection proved otherwise. God vindicated Christ's loving sacrifice and, in principle, ended the Devil's stronghold on the world. This victory forms the basis of our confidence that God will vindicate our non-common-sensical imitation of Christ. As we manifest kingdom life by replicating Jesus to the world, it may often look like we are doing little—and even sometimes look like we are losing ground. But we know, against all common sense, that nothing could be further from the truth. However trivial they may seem, we know that Christlike acts are doing more to bring the world to the glorious end God has for it than any "power over" act ever could.

Kingdom people need to see the world through the eyes of the kingdom of God, the eyes of faith, not through the eyes of the kingdom of the world. For example, to the natural eye it looks like the relative strength of two armies fighting on the battlefield determines the outcome of a battle. But the eye of faith should see that this outcome is much more affected by a man standing on a hill raising his arms in prayer (Ex. 17:8–13). Faith understands that the fate of nations may hinge more on whether a kingdom person is praying than on the decisions of its leaders (Ezek. 22:29–31).

Looking at the world in this way, a kingdom person can see the shallowness of the argument that moves from a comparatively good outcome produced through violent means to the necessity of violence to produce a good outcome. While the Civil War did produce at least one good outcome, for example, a kingdom person must see the shallowness of concluding that this outcome could *only* have been achieved by having over six hundred thousand people—most of whom professed Christ—slaughtering each other. A kingdom person should rather wonder what might have happened had more kingdom people been willing to live out the call of the radical kingdom. What might have happened if more people had trusted "power under" rather than resorting to "power over"?

How much of the violence of the Civil War could have been avoided if, say, a larger number of kingdom people were persistently and fervently in prayer to end slavery and avoid war? Such considerations are of course silly from a kingdom-of-the-world perspective, but from a kingdom of God perspective few questions could be more relevant. And how much of the bloodshed could have been avoided had more white Christians demonstrated Calvary-quality love by resisting the evil of slavery through nonviolent means?

Similarly, what if millions (rather than hundreds) of whites had been willing to "come under" black slaves by helping with the underground railroad? What if more than a miniscule number of white Christians had refused to benefit in any way from the slave trade? What if, rather than taking up arms, Christians from the North and South would have been willing to sit down together and seriously ask the kingdom question, how can we sacrifice of our own resources to make it economically feasible to Southern, white land owners to set blacks free? What if instead of fearing a loss of congregants and revenue, denominational leaders had leveraged their authority to get white pastors to treat owning slaves as seriously as the sin of, say, adultery?

In other words, what might have happened if multitudes of those who claimed to be Christian were actually Christlike? Undoubtedly, the outcome would have been much better than the "good" outcome of the war, and it would have been achieved without such a diabolical loss of life. In fact, as noted above, had sufficient numbers been willing to live out the call of the kingdom, slavery never would have been a reality in the first place.

We accept arguments about the necessity of violence because historically this is the approach that's usually been used to resolve large-scale conflicts. What is more, while military victories tend to be celebrated, nonviolent victories seem to pass without notice. Most know about Gandhi and Martin Luther King Jr., but the nonviolent revolutions that ended various unjust dictatorships and brought increased freedom to more than three billion people in the twentieth century alone are hardly ever discussed.[12]

Consequently, we are conditioned to think violence is the only viable approach to resolving conflict. Yet kingdom people are called to follow the example of Jesus, not the example of Caesar or world history. We are called to trust "power under," not "power over." And we are thereby called to show by our life that, while violence sometimes brings about some positive results, violence is never inevitable—if only kingdom people will live out their unique kingdom call.

4. DON'T YOUR IDEAS LEAD TO PASSIVITY?

Your proposal is a prescription for disaster! Like the hangman, if Christians don't aggressively fight the forces of evil in our culture, eventually we will find ourselves getting hung. The marriage of gays, for example, is a stepping stone toward outlawing our religious right to preach that homosexuality is a sin. Christians have a responsibility to take a strong public stand now to stop this slippery slope into a culture that may eventually make being a Christian illegal. You're irresponsibly encouraging Christians to sit by while we see our rights slowly erode.

A lot of this sort of "sky is falling" rhetoric is going around these days. While often spoken sincerely, it instills fear in many Christians. It is also used to motivate them to support certain political positions, policies, and candidates as the last, best hope left to the church and to America itself.

Four things need to be said in response.

First, to say that followers of Jesus should act like Jesus is not to say they should "just sit by." The objection assumes that the only alternative to seizing "power over" is doing nothing. The objection exemplifies a complete trust in worldly power and a lack of trust in kingdom power. To follow Jesus is not only to do something; it is to do something far more powerful than fighting a "power over" battle ever could. Such battles may succeed in preserving one's own rights, but it will not transform lives and advance the kingdom.

If, on the other hand, we collectively follow the example of Jesus and bleed for those who (some fear) may take away our rights—if we do not resist evil and instead do good to those who (some think) are persecuting us—this will sow kingdom seeds that will bear fruit for eternity. It is the one course of action that is not only faithful to the kingdom but contains the possibility of transforming those who (some believe) are trying to take away our rights. The kingdom of God does not seek to conquer; it seeks to transform.

Second, we need to understand that fear is a diabolic force. Its ultimate creator is Satan, and he uses it to keep us in bondage (Heb. 2:15). Throughout history, leaders have used fear to rally the masses around their causes, sometimes getting them to do things they otherwise would never dream of. Most of the worst atrocities committed in history—by so-called Christians and others—were motivated by fear. People felt threatened, demonized the ones who threatened them, and thus felt justified in doing whatever they thought necessary to protect themselves. It is impossible to live in love and live in fear at the same time, which is why Scripture says that love casts out fear (1 John 4:18).

Now, as kingdom people we are called to live in love, which means we are called and empowered to live *free of fear*. Because our source of worth, significance, and security is found exclusively in God's love and God's reign, not our own immediate well-being, and because we believe in the resurrection, we are empowered to love even those who threaten our well-being—for this does not threaten our essential worth, significance, and security. We are, therefore, not to fear them (see 1 Peter 3:14–18). If we *do* fear them, it is only because some element of our essential worth, significance, and security is rooted in what they threaten. In other words, fear is an indication that we are living in idolatry, not love.

All this is to say that kingdom people whose lives are exclusively rooted in Jesus Christ will not succumb to motivation by fear. Our motivation for all we do is to be love, not fear (1 Cor. 16:14; 2 Cor. 5:14).

Third, like most slippery slope arguments, the logic of the question posed above is highly suspect. There is no inherent connection between allowing gay unions to be termed *marriages* on the one hand, and outlawing the view that homosexuality is a sin (let alone outlawing Christianity) on the other. Now, there *is* precedent from certain countries that have allowed gay marriages for concluding that *hate speech* against homosexuals may soon be outlawed. But why should Christians be against this? To the contrary, wouldn't we find Jesus entering into solidarity with gays and others who might be the objects of hate speech? Is this not precisely what he did in befriending the tax collectors and prostitutes of his day, even though it cost him his reputation among the "socially respectable" religious people? And are we not called to imitate him in this, as in every other matter?

Nevertheless, let us suppose that the doomsday prophets are right. Let us suppose that the sky *is* falling. Suppose (as some have argued) that within ten years the government is going to make it a crime to say out loud that homosexuality is a sin. Let us suppose this will be followed (as some argue) by public evangelism being outlawed, by our Bibles being confiscated, and eventually by Christianity becoming illegal.

Should we be afraid of this? Should we rise up to protect ourselves from this slippery slope? Where do we find Jesus ever worrying about such things? When did Jesus ever concern himself with protecting his rights or the rights of the community he was founding? Did he not rather do the exact opposite and teach us to do the same? He had all the power in the universe at his disposal and had every right to use it, yet out of love he let himself be crucified. This is how he established and manifested the domain in which God is king. And we expand and manifest the domain in which God is king by imitating him in this act.

Instead of fearing the possibility of persecution someday, kingdom people should trust that if this happened, God would use it for the furthering of his kingdom, just as he used Jesus' death. In fact, as terrible as they often are, persecutions have usually had a positive kingdom effect. While gaining political power has always harmed the church, as we saw in chapter 4, persecutions have almost always served to strengthen it. Tertullian was on the mark when he said that the blood of the martyrs is the seed of the church.[13]

As much as we would hate having our religious rights taken away (let alone being thrown into prison or even martyred) it would not be too much to suggest that perhaps *this* is exactly what the American church needs! As it stands now, the American church reflects pagan American culture in almost every respect, as numerous studies have shown. The radically countercultural and revolutionary movement that Jesus birthed has, in our country (as in every other "Christian" country), been largely reduced to little more than a preservation society for a national civil religion. A persecution would cure this ill, forcing Christianity to *mean* something significant. It would force us to be the one thing we are called to be: imitators of God, dying on a cross for those who crucified him.

In the early church, Christians considered it an honor to be martyred for their faith and to testify to the loving lordship of Christ by dying the way he died. They weren't gluttons for punishment;

they simply saw their life and death from a kingdom perspective. If dying furthered the purpose of the kingdom of God, they considered it an honor. How things have changed! We now find ourselves in a version of Christianity where protecting *ourselves* is one of the main things we stand for—"in Jesus' name"! In the name of the one who surrendered his rights and died for sinners, we fight against sinners for our rights! As with many other things, we do what ordinary pagans do—we simply *Christianize* it.

"But if we lose our rights," some people object, "we lose our power to speak into people's lives and into the culture at large." In response, I simply ask, "Where is your faith?" Our power to speak into people's lives and into the culture has never been given by Caesar, and it therefore can't be taken away by Caesar. Civil religion worries about such things, but not the kingdom of God. Our power has always been our willingness to imitate Jesus, our willingness to suffer for the sake of righteousness, and our willingness to bleed for others as Christ has bled for us. It has been the availability of Caesar's power and the quasi-Christian veneer of our civil religion in America that has caused many of us to forget this.

With or without persecution, our call is to simply live in sacrificial love and trust that the sovereign God will use our love to further his kingdom, as he did with the love Jesus expressed to us and all people on Calvary.

5. DON'T WE BEST SERVE THE OPPRESSED BY OVERTHROWING THEIR OPPRESSORS?

How can we come under and serve people who are oppressed by unjust laws unless we're willing to work to gain power over those who oppress them?

Of all the questions in this chapter, I have personally struggled the most with this one. I offer three considerations that I find helpful in gaining clarity on a unique kingdom-of-God perspective on confronting unjust, oppressive laws.

First, while the kingdom of the world focuses on controlling behavior, the kingdom of God focuses on transforming hearts.

When hearts are transformed, behavior follows. Laws simply reflect the hearts of those empowered to make them. So, the focus of citizens of the kingdom of God should be on changing the hearts of oppressors rather than on trying to conquer them with a greater coercive power.

As both Mahatma Gandhi and Martin Luther King Jr. realized, the oppressors are themselves oppressed by their oppression of others. The goal of kingdom people, therefore, must be to free the oppressor from his or her oppressed heart, which in turn frees those who are oppressed by them. To accomplish this, we must first possess a genuine love and concern for the oppressors, as Gandhi and King both said. We must genuinely love our enemy, as Jesus taught. The kingdom of God is a radical way of *being* before it is a particular way of *acting* against injustice and oppression. It is about *living* in love, as Christ loved us and gave his life for us (Eph. 5:2) before it is about *acting* in a loving manner that will improve the world. And we will never be able to do the latter unless we have cultivated the former. Only to the extent that a heart and mind has been purged of "all bitterness ... wrath and anger" (Eph. 4:31) and saturated with the reign of God can a person even see the sensibility of the kingdom approach to oppression and injustice, let alone be empowered to carry it out consistently.

Second, as with everything else in the kingdom of God, we "come under" oppressors and help free them from their own oppression by being willing to replicate the Calvary-quality love of Jesus toward them. And we do this primarily by replicating the Calvary-quality love of Jesus toward those they oppress.

As we saw in chapter 6, Jesus exposed the ugliness of inhumane religious laws by healing on the Sabbath. He exposed the ugliness of patriarchy by his respectful treatment of women. He exposed the ugliness of cultural taboos by touching lepers and having close fellowship with socially unacceptable "sinners." He exposed the ugliness of institutionalized Jewish racism by ministering to and praising Gentiles and Samaritans. And he exposed the ugly injustice of the Roman government and the world by entering into solidarity with a rebel race and letting us crucify him on the cross. Jesus' whole life was the kingdom of God, and his consistent sacrificial love, in solidarity with the oppressed, consistently provided a beautiful contrast to the ugliness of the oppressive kingdom of the world and the oppressive principalities and powers that are over it.

As followers of Jesus, we are called to do the same. While we, along with all decent citizens, should work against unjust laws by political means, our distinctive calling *as kingdom people* is to go far beyond this and manifest Calvary-quality love. We are called to enter into solidarity with all who are marginalized and crushed by the powers-that-be and to allow ourselves to be marginalized and crushed along with them. This Calvary-quality love exposes the ugly injustice of laws that marginalize and crush, and in this way just possibly leads oppressors to repent.

This solidarity involves refusing to participate in and benefit from unjust, oppressive laws. Kingdom people are called to obey societal laws insofar as this is possible (Rom. 12:18; 13:1), but when obedience to the laws of the land conflict with obedience to God, the laws of the land must be broken. As Peter said, "We must obey God rather than any human authority" when the two conflict with one another (Acts 5:29). Of course, as with Jesus, this civil disobedience may bring us under the power of the sword—and *that* is the point. When we, following Jesus' example, allow ourselves to be unjustly crucified at the hands of an unjust, oppressive regime, we serve the oppressor by further exposing the ugliness of the oppressive regime. Our love for the oppressed and the oppressor heaps "burning coals on their heads" (Rom. 12:20) and puts to shame those who malign us (1 Peter 3:16).

Third, while this approach will always place self-sacrificial love at the center, it will look quite different from situation to situation. The way Gandhi united Indians and others and led them to nonviolently resist unjust British rule was different from the way King united blacks and others to nonfiolently resist unjust Jim Crow laws. What is effective in one context may not be effective in another. So kingdom people need to be "wise as serpents" in how they approach issues of injustice, just as they need to be in their approach to evangelism and all other matters (Matt. 10:16). Shrewdness is not inconsistent with the kingdom of God, for it's not inconsistent with Calvary-like love. To the contrary, the kingdom that Christ established and is now growing is a subversive move-ment that *depends* on shrewdness.

Thus, it's imperative that in any given context, confronting any given issue, kingdom people seek the "wisdom from above" (James 3:17). This is the kind of wisdom Jesus always manifested in his dealings with the religious authorities of his day, and the kind of wisdom both Gandhi and King consistently exhibited in dealing with the oppressive, unjust regimes they confronted. It's the kind of wisdom Oskar Shindler exhibited in rescuing over a thousand Jews from certain death in Nazi Germany—without violence—and Paul Rusesabagina exhibited in protecting over a thousand Tutsis from Hutu genocide in Rwanda—again, without violence. It's a godly wisdom that is willing to suffer for others and that can discern the most effective way of doing this. It's a wisdom that effectively manifests the life and love of the kingdom of God, while exposing the demonic dimension of the kingdom of the world.

Of course, many have argued that this approach is naive when one is dealing with evil people empowered to make and enforce evil laws. Such people cannot hope to be converted, it is argued: they must be overpowered. This is the very kind of thinking that was behind Peter's use of the sword and that has fueled the bloody "power over" merry-go-round throughout history. It is, sadly, the staple of the way all versions of the kingdom of the world oper-ate. Yet from a kingdom-of-God perspective, we must simply con-clude that if it's naive to think there is an alternative "power under" way of addressing issues and changing the world, then so be it. The attitude of the kingdom-of-God citizen has to be that we'd rather lose by naively following a Calvary-like approach to issues than win while trusting the "power over" approach to issues.

While our goal is to be faithful rather than pragmatic, experience has shown that Christ's approach, while costly, is often effective

—the liberation of India from oppressive British rule and the acquisition of civil rights for blacks in America being the two most noteworthy examples. But even when it looks like this approach doesn't work, even when it looks like evil triumphs by putting us and others to death, the kingdom person is to remember that it's still a "Good Friday" world. We are to have faith that things will look different when Easter morning arrives. The ultimate hope of the world is not found in achieving victory now. The ultimate hope of the world is the resurrection, when all things shall be reconciled to God (Col. 1:20). Then we will see that no act of kingdom love has ever been wasted.

In the meantime, faithfulness to our Lord rather than carnal effectiveness in gaining the upper hand in the affairs of the world is to be our guide.

ACKNOWLEDGMENTS

THIS BOOK WOULD NEVER HAVE BEEN WRITTEN WITHOUT THE LOVE, support, and input of many people. First, I have to thank the radical kingdom people of Woodland Hills Church in Maplewood, Minnesota, whom I have had the honor of pastoring for the last thirteen years. This book arose out of a controversial six-week sermon series I preached in the spring of 2004 entitled "The Cross and the Sword." I know better now than I did back then that this message was (and is) not an easy one for many American evangelicals to hear, for it calls into question assumptions about "God and country" that have been part of American culture from the time Christian Europeans first conquered this land.

Yet the majority of this highly unusual American megachurch hung in there and wrestled with the issues. Indeed, the love and support I received from my congregation during and after this difficult series was overwhelming. It is a joy to serve people who are willing to allow their allegiance to Christ to call into question every aspect of their culture—even, and especially, aspects that may be near and dear to their hearts. This is what the kingdom of God is all about! *Thank you for hanging in there!*

While I cannot begin to name all those who contributed to this book, several have to be mentioned. Gail ("spunky") Wolf offered invaluable help at the initial stages, transcribing and editing the initial sermons. My dear ultraliberal friend Joanne Arnold, my dear ultraconservative friend James Inkeep, my dear confused-in-the-middle friend Paul Eddy, and my dear supremely balanced friend Jay Barnes each read the manuscript at various stages and offered insightful, critical feedback. Not only this, but the support and feedback given by the entire editorial staff of Zondervan was simply amazing. *I thank you all!*

I also have to express my love and appreciation to the covenant community I have "done life" with the last ten years—Julie and Alex Ross, Terri and Dave Churchhill, and Marcia and Greg Erickson (along with all our lovely children and pets). All my ideas have to some extent been shaped by the friendly—yet "animated"—debate that regularly takes place in this rare and precious community of friends. Of course, I also need to say, from the very depths of my heart, that neither this nor any other book I've written would have been possible without the sacrificial love and support of my lifelong friend and wife, Shelley ("Beso") Boyd. *How I love you!*

Finally, though she played no role in the formation of this book—indeed, for all I know, she may have serious disagreements with it—I have to express my deepest, heartfelt appreciation for my stepmother, Jeanne Boyd, to whom this book is dedicated. For a variety of tragic reasons, my father was a cynical, depressed, alcohol-abusing atheist until he married Jeanne. I'm convinced that her understanding, patience, and amazing love not only made the last decades of his life his happiest, but softened his heart and paved the way for him to accept Christ in the last years of his life. How does a son begin to thank a person for doing *that*? The dedication of this book to you is an inadequate but sincere token. *Words come to an end here.*

NOTES

INTRODUCTION: HOW THIS BOOK CAME TO BE — AND WHY IT MAY IRRITATE SOME READERS

1. Approximately seven hundred left during the six-week "Cross and the Sword" sermon series. Another three hundred or so left when I "didn't have the good sense" to back off the topic but rather returned to it once again just prior to the election.

2. By *myth* I mean "a story that speaks of meaning and purpose, and for this reason it speaks truth to those who take it seriously." Richard T. Hughs, *Myths Americans Live By* (Urbana and Chicago: University of Illinois, 2004), 2.

3. For two excellent treatments of this dimension of American mythic history, see Richard Jewett and John Shelton Lawrence, *Captain America and the Crusade against Evil* (Grand Rapids, Mich.: Eerdmans, 2003); and Hughs, *Myths Americans Live By*. As shall become clear later on, the American myth is simply a version of a myth that has dominated Christianity since the fourth century when Christianity emerged from its persecuted past and "triumphed" as a global force. From Constantine on, the church has more often than not seen itself as the religious guardian of the empire—with disastrous consequences for the gospel *and often for the empire*.

4. Other factors contribute to the increased political activism of American evangelicals. For example, 9/11 obviously increased patriotism nationwide. What's more, since the 1970s, after years of lying dormant, evangelicals have experienced the political clout they wield when they speak with a united voice.

5. Following Revelations 11:15, I shall speak of the kingdom of the world as a single kingdom because, as we shall see, in a spiritual sense all earthly governments are part of one kingdom that is ruled by Satan (cf. Luke 4:6–7). I should also note that the "kingdom of the world" isn't *only* about governments. It is manifested on a personal, societal, and global level whenever we try to advance our own interests at the

expense of others' interests, thus exercising "power over" them. In this work, however, I am centrally concerned with governmental manifestations of the kingdom of the world and how Christians are to relate to it.

6. For an excellent critique of "the Christian left" along the theological lines put forth in their books, see Vernard Eller's *Christian Anarchy: Jesus' Primacy over the Powers* (Grand Rapids, Mich.: Eerdmans, 1987). Unfortunately I happened upon Eller's work only just before to the publication of this book and thus was unable to integrate it into my own.

7. This paragraph could be read as assuming that all Christians actively participate in the political process by voting or by other means. Some Christians, of course, choose to abstain from this participation as a matter of principle. Following the example of Jesus, they have decided that they have no business trying to improve the world by political means of any sort. Moreover, some point out, quite rightly, that all participation in political processes involves *compromise*. As kingdom people, they refuse to choose between competing compromising positions. While I myself continue to participate in the political process, I want to register my sympathies for this position (which is not to be confused with abstaining from participation out of apathy).

CHAPTER 1: THE KINGDOM OF THE SWORD

1. Stanley Hauerwas and William Willimon, *Resident Aliens: Life in a Christian Colony* (Nashville: Abingdon, 1989), 62.

2. John Howard Yoder, *The Politics of Jesus* (Grand Rapids, Mich.: Eerdmans, 2nd ed. 1994 [1972]), 201–2. Another insightful discussion of Romans 13 is found in Eller, *Christian Anarchy*.

3. See Barbara R. Rossing, *The Choice between Two Cities: Whore, Bride, and Empire in the Apocalypse* (Harrisburg, Penn; Trinity, 1999); Christopher Rowland, "The Book of Revelation," in *New Interpreter's Bible*, vol. 12 (Nashville: Abingdon, 1998), 685–86; D. E. Aune, *Revelation 17–22* of the World Bible Commentary 52C (Nashville: Nelson, 1998), 960–61.

4. Yoder has an excellent discussion of the powers as they relate to the structure of societies in *The Politics of Jesus*, chapter 8. Though he overly demythologizes "the powers" in my estimation, Walter Wink's series on *The Powers* is very informative and insightful. See Walter Wink, *Naming the Powers* (Philadelphia: Fortress, 1984); *Unmasking*

the Powers (Philadelphia: Fortress, 1986); *Engaging the Powers* (Minneapolis: Fortress, 1992). See also Hendrikus Berkhof, *Christ and the Powers* (Scottdale, Penn.: Herald, 1962); G. B. Caird, *Principalities and Powers* (Oxford: Clarendon, 1956) and Gregory Boyd, *God at War: The Bible and Spiritual Conflict* (Downers Grove, Ill.: InterVarsity, 2001).

5. See Wink, *Engaging the Powers*, 13–31. Wink traces the origins of the myth to Babylon and argues that the violent religion of Babylon, "not Christianity, is the real religion of America" (13). The essence of the religion is the belief that violence can redeem us and exterminate evil rather than simply perpetuate it.

CHAPTER 2: THE KINGDOM OF THE CROSS

1. See, for example, G. R. Beasley-Murray, *Jesus and the Kingdom of God* (Grand Rapids, Mich.: Eerdmans, 1986); B. Chilton, *Pure Kingdom: Jesus' Vision of God* (Grand Rapids, Mich.: Eerdmans, 1996); R. Horsely, *Jesus and Empire: The Kingdom of God and the New World Disorder* (Minneapolis: Fortress, 2003); E. Maloney, *Jesus' Urgent Message for Today: The Kingdom of God in Mark's Gospel* (New York: Continuum, 2004).

2. See Gregory Boyd, "The Christus Victor View of the Atonement," in *Four Views of the Atonement*, eds. P. Eddy and J. Bielby (Downers Grove, Ill: InterVarsity, 2006). Here I argue that Jesus' life, teachings, ministry, death, and resurrection are all centered on overthrowing Satan and the powers.

3. For example, according to Acts, so closely does Jesus identify himself with his "body" that he regards Paul's persecution of Christians as a persecution of him (Acts 9:1–4). On the close identification of the church as the "body of Christ" with Christ in Paul's theology, see J. Dunn, *The Theology of Paul the Apostle* (Grand Rapids, Mich.: Eerdmans, 1998), 548–52.

4. Under the influence of the dispensational/rapture theology that has taken evangelicalism by storm over the last hundred years, many Christians are expecting God to take Christians *out of* the world and then destroy the earth. Heaven, they believe, is "located" somewhere else. Scripture, however, is consistent in its witness that God will not abandon the earth. The kingdom of God will be established *on a renewed earth* (for example, 2 Peter 3:13; Rev. 5:10; 21:1–3). On the errors and dangers of the dispensational view, see Barbara R. Rossing, *The*

Rapture Exposed (Boulder, Colo.: Westview, 2004), esp. 141–58. See also Norman C. Habel, ed. *Readings from the Perspective of the Earth* (Sheffield, England: Sheffield Academic Press, 2002) and Catherine Keller, *God and Power: Counter-Apocalyptic Journeys* (Minneapolis: Fortress, 1005). We shall discuss dispensational theology further in chapter 4.

5. See Rossing, *Rapture Exposed*, 109–22; Yoder, *The Politics of Jesus*, chap. 12, "The War of the Lamb." See also Ward Ewing, *The Power of the Lamb: Revelation's Theology of Liberation for You* (Cambridge, Mass.: Cowley Press, 1990).

6. For a full discussion, see Boyd, *God at War*, chap. 9; and Boyd, "The Christus Victor View."

7. "The cross," writes Hauerwas, "is the summary of his whole life." S. Hauerwas, *Peaceable Kingdom* (South Bend, Ind.: University of Notre Dame, 1983), 76.

8. Yoder, *Politics of Jesus*, 235.

9. Lee C. Camp, *Mere Discipleship: Radical Christianity in a Rebellious World* (Grand Rapids, Mich.: Braznos, 2003), 94.

10. See Walter Wink, *Jesus and Nonviolence: A Third Way* (Minneapolis: Fortress, 2003), 13–27.

11. Martin Luther King Jr., *Stride toward Freedom* (New York: Harper & Row, 1958), 103–4. For Gandhi's own translation of *Satyagraha*, see Mahatma Gandhi, *The Collected Works of Mahatma Gandhi* (New Delhi: Navajivan Trust, Ahmedabad, 1961), 10:64. On Jesus' influence on Gandhi, see Michael Battle's insightful discussion in *Blessed Are the Peacemakers: A Christian Spirituality of Nonviolence* (Macon, Ga.: Mercer University Press, 2004), chap. 3.

12. Hauerwas and Willimon, *Resident Aliens*, 84.

13. Ibid., 85–86.

14. For an excellent discussion of the unique kingdom community Jesus came to establish as expressed in Matthew 5, see Richard Hays, *The Moral Vision of the New Testament: Community, Cross, New Creation* (San Francisco: HarperSanFrancisco, 1996), 319–29. Hays writes, for example, that

> the kingdom of God as figured forth in Matthew 5 is full of surprises. Matthew offers a vision of a radical countercultural community of discipleship characterized by a "higher righteousness"—a community free of anger, lust, falsehood, and violence. The transcendence of violence through loving the enemy is the most salient feature of this new model

polis.... Instead of wielding the power of violence, the community of Jesus' disciples is to be meek, merciful, pure, devoted to peacemaking, and willing to suffer persecution—and blessed precisely in its faithfulness to this paradoxical vision. (322)

15. According to Scripture, suffering is to be expected by all who follow Jesus (1 Peter 2:20–21; 3:14–18). Carrying the cross is essential to discipleship (Luke 14:27–33). Indeed, when disciples suffer they participate in the suffering and death of Christ (2 Cor. 1:5; 4:10; Phil. 1:20; Col. 1:24; 1 Peter 4:12–16). "The believer's cross is, like that of Jesus, the price of social nonconformity." Yoder, *Politics of Jesus*, 96; cf. 120–27. As Bonhoeffer noted: "Suffering ... is the badge of true discipleship. The disciple is not above his master." Dietrich Bonhoeffer, *The Cost of Discipleship* (New York: Simon and Shuster, 1995), 91. The church is called to be a "cruciform church," as Leonard Allen put it. All we are about in one form or another manifests Calvary. We are called to sacrifice and thus on a variety of levels suffer for the advancement of God's reign. See C. Leonard Allen, *The Cruciform Church: Becoming a Cross-Shaped People in a Secular World* (Abilene, Tex.: Abilene Christian University Press, 1990).

CHAPTER 3: KEEPING THE KINGDOM HOLY

1. Dietrich Bonhoeffer, *Ethics* (New York: Touchstone, 1995 [1949]), 350.
2. Yoder, *The Politics of Jesus*, 38.
3. Eberhard Arnold, *Writings Selected with an Introduction by Johann Christoph Arnold* (Maryknoll, N.Y.: Orbis, 2000), 41–42. Arnold goes so far as to call the church a "second incarnation." Ibid., 143.
4. Hauerwas, *Peaceable Kingdom*, 82.
5. John the Baptist's critique of Herod (Luke 3:19) does not constitute an exception to this once we understand it in its cultural context. We shall discuss this in chapter 7.
6. Bonhoeffer, *Ethics*, 350.
7. Andre Trocme, *Jesus and the Non-Violent Revolution* (Farmington, Penn.: The Bruderhof Foundation, 2004), 53.
8. Camp, *Mere Discipleship*, 105.
9. In some regions the Jewish outrage against coins bearing the emperor's image was so great the government minted special coins without this image. See the discussion in G. Boyd and P. Eddy, *The Jesus Legend* (Grand Rapids, Mich.: Baker Book, 2006), chap. 2.

10. Eller's comment is relevant: "A prime characteristic of wordly politics is its invariable framing of itself as an 'adversarial contest.' There has to be a battle. One party, ideology, cause, group, lobby, or power bloc which has designated itself as 'the Good, the True, and the Beautiful' sets out to overbear, overwhelm, overcome, overpower, or otherwise impose itself on whatever opposing parties think *they* deserve the title." And it is "a power contest among the morally pretentious." *Christian Anarchy*, xii.

11. Trocme, *Non-Violent Revolution*, 132.

CHAPTER 4: FROM RESIDENT ALIENS TO CONQUERING WARLORDS

1. Rev. Jerry Falwell, CNN *Late Edition with Wolf Blitzer*, October 24, 2004.

2. C. S. Lewis, *Mere Christianity*, (New York: Macmillian, 1960 [1943]), 51.

3. On the already–not yet tension of the New Testament, see Werner Georg Kümmel, *Promise and Fulfillment: The Eschatological Message of Jesus*, trans. D. M. Barton (London: SCM, 3d ed. 1961); George E. Ladd, *The Presence of the Future* (Grand Rapids, Mich.: Eerdmans, 1974).

4. Paul refers to believers as "fellow workers" of God (1 Cor. 3:9; 2 Cor. 6:1). The people of Meroz were cursed "because they did not come to the help of the LORD, to the help of the LORD against the mighty" (Judg. 5:23). The trinitarian God has chosen to create a world in which he often relies on intermediaries to carry out his will. Humans were—and yet are—intended to be God's viceroys upon the earth, bringing about God's will "on earth as it is in heaven" (Matt. 6:10). See E. Sauer, *The King of the Earth* (Palm Springs: Ronald N. Hayes Publishers, reprint 1981); D. G. McCartney, "Ecce Homo: The Coming of the Kingdom as the Restoration of Human Viceregency," *Westminster Theological Journal* 56 (1994): 1–21; G. Boyd, *God at War: The Bible and Spiritual Conflict* (Downers Grove, Ill.: InterVarsity, 1997), 110–12.

5. On Satan's warfare upon the church and the world after the resurrection, see Boyd, *God at War*, chap. 10.

6. Hauerwas and Willimon, *Resident Aliens*, 12.

7. For an overview of the misguided exegesis and political dangers of this movement, see B. R. Rossing, *The Rapture Exposed: The Message of Hope in the Book of Revelation* (Boulder, Colo.: Westview, 2004).

Tony Campolo also has a good discussion on the non-Christian and potentially cataclysmic implications of dispensationalism in *Speaking My Mind* (Nashville: W, 2004), 210–23. See also Jewett and Lawrence, *Captain America.*

8. On the domination system, see W. Wink, *Engaging the Powers* (Minneapolis: Fortress, 1992).

9. Yoder, *The Politics of Jesus*, 51 (emphasis added).

10. John MacKensie captures the point when he notes that Satan's offer is not rejected "because Satan is unable to deliver what he promises; it is rejected because secular power is altogether inept for the mission of Jesus, indeed because the use of secular power is hostile to his mission." John MacKensie, *Authority in the Church* (New York: Sheed and Ward, 1966), 29. Yoder insightfully discusses how both the incarnation and crucifixion reveal that Jesus chose faithfulness to God's character over "effectiveness" in managing the world. *Politics of Jesus*, 228–37. Disciples of Jesus are called to do the same. Tragically, as we shall see shortly, the church has more often than not chosen effectiveness over faithfulness. For a brilliant discussion of how Christians (and others) degenerate into evil when we choose efficiency over faithfulness, see Camp, *Mere Discipleship*, 30–39.

11. Camp, *Mere Discipleship*, 54.

12. Early church theologians often argued that the biblical promises for the "new world" that the Messiah would bring about—the world where violence has ended and love reigns—are fulfilled in their new community. The undeniability of this fact functioned as evidence for Christ's lordship. See, for example, Justin, "Dialogue with Trypho," *Ante-Nicene Fathers*, eds. Alexander Roberts and James Donaldson (Peabody, Mass.: Hendrickson, 1999 [1885]), vol. 1, 254; Tertullian, "An Answer to Jews," *Ante-Nicene Fathers*, vol. 1, 154; Origen, "Against Celsus," *Ante-Nicene Fathers*, vol. 4, 558. For a classic overview of Christian attitudes toward war throughout history, highlighting the uniform pacifism of the early church, see Roland H. Bainton, *Christian Attitudes toward War and Peace* (Nashville: Abingdon, 1960).

13. H. R. Loyn and J. Percival, eds. and trans., *The Reign of Charlemagne: Documents on Carolingian Government and Administration* (New York: St. Martins, 1975), 52. For overviews of Christendom's rise to power, see J. N. Hillgarth, *The Conversion of Western Europe* (Englewood Cliffs, N.J.: Prentice Hall, 1969), and R. A. Markus, *The End of Ancient Christianity* (Cambridge: Cambridge University, 1990).

14. See W. H. C. Frend, *The Donatist Church* (Oxford: Clarendon, 1952); J. E. Merdinger, *Rome and the African Church in the Time of Augustine* (New Haven, Conn.: Yale University), chaps. 2 and 3. There were other theological and sociological factors that separated Donatists from Catholics as well.

15. C. Kirwan (*Augustine* [London: Routledge, 1989]) provides a succinct summary and citation of various sources (214 ff.). See also P. Brown, *Augustine of Hippo* (Berkley and Los Angeles, Calif.: University of California 1967), chaps. 19–21. W. H. C. Frend notes that it was during the Donatist controversy that "the Lucan text, 'Compel them to come in,' was invoked [by Augustine] to justify the use of force with the gravest consequences for the future of Christian brotherhood and toleration." W. H. Frend, *The Early Church* (Philadelphia, PA: Fortress, 1982), 204.

16. For overviews, see W. Sumner Davis, *Heretics: The Bloody History of the Church* (La Verne, Tenn.: Lightning Source, 2002); G. G. Coulton, *Inquisition and Liberty* (Glouster, Mass.: Peter Smith, 1969); James A. Haught, *Holy Horrors* (Buffalo: Prometheus, 1990); Henry Charles Lea, *The Inquisition of the Middle Ages*, abridged by Margaret Nicholson (New York: Macmillan, 1961). The classic text on the persecution of Christian groups not aligned with the official church is Thieleman J. van Braght, *The Martyr's Mirror: The Story of Seventeen Centuries of Christian Martyrdom, from the Time of Christ to AD 1660* (Scottdale, Penn.: Herald, 14th Eng. ed., 1985 [1660]). For various assessments of the church's violent tradition, see Kenneth R. Chase and Alan Jacobs, eds., *Must Christianity Be Violent?* (Grand Rapids, Mich.: Braznos, 2003).

17. Previous estimates were in the millions, but while some still continue to defend such estimates (Andrea Dworkin, *Woman Hating: A Radical Look at Sexuality* [New York: Dutton, 1974]) more recent scholarship has arrived at estimates closer to a hundred thousand. On the persecution of witches, see Norman Cohn, *Europe's Inner Demons* (Chicago: University of Chicago, rev. ed. 2000 [1975]); Brian Levack, *The Witch Hunt in Early Modern Europe* (London: Longman, 2nd ed. 1995); and Robin Briggs, *Witches and Neighbors: The Social and Cultural Content of European Witchcraft* (New York: Penguin, 1998). For two superb accounts of the church's tragic treatment of Jews throughout history, see J. Carroll, *Constantine's Sword: The Church and the Jews* (Boston/New York: Houghton Mifflin, 2001) and David Rausch, *A Legacy of*

Hatred: Why Christian Must Not Forget the Holocaust (Chicago: Moody, 1984).

18. For example, a 1493 Papal Bull justified declaring war on any native South Americans who refused to adhere to Christianity. In defense of this stance, the jurist Encisco claimed in 1509: "The king has every right to send his men to the Indies to demand their territory from these idolaters because he had received it from the pope. If the Indians refuse, he may quite legally fight them, kill them and enslave them, just as Joshua enslaved the inhabitants of the country of Canaan." Jean Delumeau, *Catholicism between Luther and Voltaire* (London: Burns and Oats, 1977), 85.

19. See Ernest Lee Tuveson, *Redeemer Nation* (Chicago: University of Chicago, 1968) and R. P. Beaver, "Missionary Motivation through Three Centuries," in *Reinterpretation in American Church History*, ed. Jerald C. Brauer (Chicago: University of Chicago, 1968). For an insightful account of how missionaries were used, often unwittingly, in the exploitation and genocide of native Americans, see George E. Tinker, *Missionary Conquest* (Minneapolis: Fortress, 1993). Perhaps the most famous and most informative firsthand account of barbarism carried out by early American settlers is provided by Las Casas, a priest who was part of Colombus's expedition and provided a trenchant critique of his exploits. See G. Gutiérrez, *Las Casas: In Search of the Poor of Jesus Christ*, trans. R. Barr (Maryknoll, N.Y.: Orbis, 1995); David M. Traboulay, *Columbus and Las Casas: The Conquest and Christianization of America, 1492–1566* (New York: University Press of America, 1994).

CHAPTER 5: TAKING AMERICA BACK FOR GOD

1. Leo Tolstoy, *The Kingdom of God Is within You* (Lincoln and London: University of Nebraska, 1984 [1894]), 344.

2. Camp, *Mere Discipleship*, 43.

3. See chapter 9 for a discussion on difficulties surrounding a Christian assessment of whether a war is just or not.

4. The claim to having purely altruistic and righteous motives when going into war has been a staple of American politics and culture. Jewett and Lawrence show how this is rooted in the mythic understanding of America as God's new Israel and the righteous "city set on a hill." For a comprehensive historic analysis and insightful critique, see Jewett and Lawrence, *Captain America and the Crusade against Evil* as well as Hughs, *Myths America Lives By*, esp. chap. 6.

5. While the intensity with which some strands of evangelicalism are fusing religious ideals with nationalistic ideals today is arguably unprecedented, American Christianity has tended in this direction from the start. For an excellent overview, see Jewett and Lawrence, *Captain America* as well as E. L. Tuveson, *Redeemer Nation* (Chicago: University of Chicago, 1968). See also Pat Apel, *Nine Great American Myths* (Brentwood, Tenn.: Wolgemuth & Hyatt, 1991).

6. On the origin and history of the myth of America as a Christian nation as well as the positive and negative effects it has had, see Hughs, *Myths America Lives By*, chap. 3.

7. Trocme, *Jesus and the Non-Violent Revolution*, 53.

8. Yoder, *The Politics of Jesus*, 238.

9. Yoder, *The Politics of Jesus*, 234.

10. A host of difficult questions concerning the ethics of how Christians should and should not participate in government could be raised at this point. For example, are there ways of participating in government that are inherently anti-Christian and thus wrong for Christians to engage in? On one extreme, the Lutheran tradition has tended to hold that, while all ways of participating in government are non-Christian, no way of participating in the government is necessarily anti-Christian, for one is wearing a completely different hat when one participates in government and thus is playing by an entirely different set of rules. Thus, for example, there would be no intrinsic conflict of interests with a Christian ruling a land or serving in the military, even though these offices may require one to directly or indirectly participate in killing others, thus contradicting Jesus' teaching about loving ones enemies and never returning violence with violence. On the other extreme, the early Anabaptist tradition has generally taught that all ways of participating in government are essentially anti-Christian, for they all at the very least involve compromising kingdom-of-God principles. And of course, there are a number of positions that attempt to mediate between these two extremes. Entering into this labyrinth of issues would take us too far afield from the central concern in this book (though I will address the issue of Christians and the military in chapter 9). My present concern is much more minimalistic; namely, to help Christians see that however they participate in government, it does not express their unique authority as kingdom-of-God participants, though it must of course be informed by their faith and values as a kingdom-of-God participant.

11. For a superb, trenchant critique of the myth of a Christian nation, as well as related myths America lives by, see Hughs, *Myths America Lives By*. One of the reasons American evangelicalism is so thoroughly divided between whites and nonwhites is because so much of white American evangelicalism buys strongly into American myths that have marginalized and oppressed nonwhites.

12. Arguably, in many respects America was less moral in the past than it is today. See Tony Campolo's interesting discussion in *Speaking My Mind* (Nashville, Tenn.: W, 2004), 187–201.

13. For example, in a treatise with Tripoli (now Libya), John Adams wrote that "the government of the United States of America is not, in any sense, founded on the Christian religion." The treaty, with this wording, was ratified by more than two thirds of the U.S. Senate and signed by John Adams. William McLoughlin, *Soul Liberty: The Baptists' Struggle in New England, 1630–1833* (Hanover, N.H.: Brown University, 1991), 249. It is of significance that many in the eighteenth and nineteenth centuries fought against the secularism of the Constitution, believing that America *should* be a Christian nation. See Hughs, *Myths America Lives By*, chap. 3. Several balanced assessments of the faith of the founding fathers and the role of religion in American history are Frank Lambert, *The Founding Fathers and the Place of Religion in America* (Princeton, N.J.: Princeton University, 2003); Norman Cousins, *The Republic of Reason: The Personal Philosophies of the Founding Fathers* (San Francisco: Harper & Row, 1988); Alf Mapp Jr., *The Faith of Our Fathers* (Oxford: Rowman & Littlefield, 2003); Corwin E. Smidt, *In God We Trust?: Religion and American Political Life* (Grand Rapids, Mich.: Baker, 2001); Mark Noll, *Religion and American Politics: From the Colonial Period to the 1980s* (New York/Oxford: Oxford University, 1990); Mark Noll, *One Nation Under God?: Christian Faith and Political Action in America* (San Francisco: Harper & Row, 1988). Several works representing the view that America was founded as a Christian nation are Peter Marshall and David Manuel, *The Light and the Glory* (Old Tappan, N.J.: Fleming H. Revell, 1977); Tim LaHaye, *Faith of Our Founding Fathers* (Green Forest, Ark.: Master Books, 1994), and Pat Robertson, *America's Dates with Destiny* (Nashville, Tenn.: Nelson, 1986).

14. Frederick Douglass, *Narrative of the Life of Frederick Douglass, an American Slave, Written by Himself* (New York: Signet, 1968 [1845]), 120.

CHAPTER 6: THE MYTH OF A CHRISTIAN NATION

1. Robert Bellah, "Civil Religion in America," *Dædalus, Journal of the American Academy of Arts and Sciences* 96 (Winter 1967): 1, 1–21.

2. See the PBS *Frontline* special, "The Jesus Factor." Bush's identification of America with Jesus is often subtle, but frequent. When, for example, Bush says, "Around the world, the nations must choose. They are with us, or they're with the terrorists," he is clearly echoing Jesus' teaching that "whoever is not with me is against me" (Luke 11:23). See George W. Bush, "Advancing the Cause of Freedom," speech delivered April 17, 2001. So too, when Bush declares, "There's power, *wonder-working power* in the goodness and idealism and faith of the American people," he's clearly putting America where the old Gospel hymn placed "the blood of the Lamb." See George Bush, *2002 State of the Union Address,* cited in "Bush and God," Newsweek (March 10, 2003). Such rhetoric uses religious capital to justify demonizing the enemy as evil. On Bush's religious rhetoric, see K. Lawton, "President Bush's Religious Rhetoric," *Religion and Ethics News Weekly* (February 7, 2003); A. McFeatters, "Religious Leaders Uneasy with Bush's Religious Rhetoric," *Post-Gazette National Bureau* (February 12, 2003); and J. Dart, "Bush's Religious Rhetoric Riles Critics," *Christian Century* (March 8, 2003). On Bush's effective use of religion in general, see *George W. Bush: Faith in the White House,* DVD (New York: Good Times Home Video, 2004).

3. As Robert Jewett and John Shelton Lawrence show, the use of messianic rhetoric, depicting America as the savior of the world—the "Captain America" image as they call it—has preceded every conflict America has gotten involved in. Their work not only thoroughly documents this persistent fusion of the cross and the sword but shows how it has had, and continues to have, harmful and dangerous consequences in U.S. foreign relations. See Jewett and Lawrence, *Captain America and the Crusade against Evil.* See also Hughs *Myths America Lives By,* who fleshes out the interrelated myths of America as a chosen nation, a Christian nation, a millennial nation, and an innocent nation—all of which feed into this dangerous mindset that we are always on the side of good and God while our enemies are on the side of evil and Satan.

4. President Bush expressed his bewilderment when he said, "I'm amazed that there's such misunderstanding of what our country is about that people would hate us ... like most Americans, I just can't believe it because I know how good we are. And we've got to do a better job of

making our case." "This is a Different Kind of War," *Los Angeles Times* (October 12, 2001), A16, cited in Hughs, *Myths America Lives By*, 8. Hughs argues that the bewilderment is rooted in "the myth of an innocent nation," which is closely related to the myth that America is a "chosen" and a "Christian" nation. See ibid., chaps. 1 and 3. Catherine Keller also has an insightful discussion in her *God and Power*, 18ff. For sources discussing some of the international activity of the United States that reveal the delusion of the myth of innocence and help explain some of the animosity many have toward the United States, see Mark L. Taylor, *Religion, Politics and the Christian Right* (Minneapolis: Fortress, 2005), 21.

5. Gail Gehrig defines civil religion as "the religious symbol system which relates the citizen's role and ... society's place in space, time, and history to the conditions of ultimate existence and meaning." G. Gehrig, *American Civil Religion: An Assessment* (Storrs, Conn.: Society for the Scientific Study of Religion, 1981), 18. R. Bellah, "Civil Religion in America," 1–21; See also D. G. Jones and R. E. Richey, *American Civil Religion* (San Francisco: Harper & Row, 1974). See also Apel, *Nine Great Myths*, chap. 11.

6. "Faith Has a Limited Effect on Most People's Behavior," Barna Group Research (*www.barna.org*). Even evangelicals generally differ little from the culture in terms of their basic values and behaviors. See Ron Sider, *The Scandal of the Evangelical Conscience: Why Are Christians Living Just Like the Rest of the World?* (Grand Rapids, Mich.: Baker, 2005).

7. Further problems the myth of a Christian nation creates for evangelism will be discussed in chapter 8.

8. Søren Kierkegaard, *Provocations: Spiritual Writings of Kierkegaard*, ed. C. E. Moore (Farmington, Penn.: Plough, 1999), 232. The whole of Kierkegaard's *Attack Upon "Christendom,"* ed. Walter Lowrie (Princeton, N.J.: Princeton University, 1968) is relevant to this point. The worse distortion of Christianity is not found in those who have enough passion to twist it in certain directions. It is found when Christianity loses all passion by becoming little more than the religious dimension of a culture.

9. For a discussion on questions surrounding the rationale, power, and effectiveness of prayer, see G. Boyd, *Is God to Blame? Moving Beyond Pat Answers to the Question of Suffering* (Downers Grove, Ill.: InterVarsity, 2003).

10. On God's responsiveness to prayer, see Robert Ellis, *Answering God: Towards a Theology of Intercession* (Waynesboro, Ga.: Paternoster, 2005); Vincent Brummer, *What Are We Doing When We Pray?* (London: SCM, 1984); G. Boyd, *God of the Possible* (Grand Rapids, Mich.: Baker Book, 2000).

11. Yoder, *The Politics of Jesus.* For example, Yoder argues that Jesus' ministry cannot properly be called "apolitical," for in calling it this one denies "the powerful ... impact on society of the creation of an alternative social group. It is to overrate both the power and the manageability of those particular social structures identified as 'political.' ... *Because* Jesus' particular way of rejecting the sword and at the same time condemning those who wielded it was politically relevant, both the Sanhedrin and the Procurator had to deny him the right to live, in the name of both of their forms of political responsibility.... Jesus' way is not less but more relevant to the question of how society moves than is the struggle for possession of the levers of command; to this Pilate and Caiaphas testify by their judgment on him," 106–7. See also Wink, *Engaging the Powers.*

12. On the work of Christ unmasking the powers, see W. Wink, *The Powers That Be* (New York: Doubleday, 1998); W. Wink, *Unmasking the Powers* (Philadelphia: Fortress, 1986); item., *Engaging the Powers*; Hendrikus Berkhof, *Christ and the Powers* (Scottdale, Penn.: Herald, 1962), 30–31. For an overview of how every aspect of Jesus' life was a socially relevant act of warfare against the principality and powers, see Boyd, "The Christus Victor View of the Atonement," in *Four Views of the Atonement.*

13. For fuller discussion on this, see G. Boyd, *Repenting of Religion: Turning from Judgment to the Love of God* (Grand Rapids, Mich.: Baker, 2004).

CHAPTER 7: WHEN CHIEF SINNERS BECOME MORAL GUARDIANS

1. This of course does not rule out intervention in crisis situations where, say, one person is inflicting bodily harm on another. The purpose of such an intervention obviously is not to point out the shortcomings of the attacker—to judge—but to rescue the person being attacked.

2. On this, see Boyd, *Repenting of Religion*, chap. 12.

3. For a full discussion of judgment as "the original sin" that blocks God's central purpose for creating the world (expressing and replicating the love he is), see G. Boyd, *Repenting of Religion.* As discussed in this

work, the prohibition on judgments does not preclude "discernment." We can and must distinguish between helpful and harmful behaviors and the like (Heb. 5:14). But we must never separate ourselves from people by comparing and contrasting ourselves with them.

4. Research conducted by the Barna Group (*www.barna.org*).

5. David Crary, "Bible Belt Leads U.S. in Divorces," *Associated Press* (November 12, 1999); W. D'Antonio, "Walking the Walk on Family Values," *The Boston Globe* (October 31, 2004); the Barna Group, "Born-Again Christians Just as Likely to Divorce as Are Non-Christians," *www.barna.org*.

6. Romans 2:1–10 bears reading at this point.

7. Many contemporary Christians are surprised to learn the church has historically never had a consensus of opinion on these questions.

8. Names have been changed to preserve the anonymity of the people involved.

CHAPTER 8: ONE NATION UNDER GOD?

1. Camp, *Mere Discipleship*, 94.

2. The association of America with Israel—not Jesus—has been a powerful cultural force in America from its inception. See Hughs, *Myths America Lives By* (Urbana and Chicago: University of Illinois Press, 2004), especially chap.3. Some took the parallel between America and Israel so far as to suggest that Native Americans were literally descendents of the Canaanites and that God had ordained their conquest, if not extermination, just as he had in the days of Joshua. Rev. Ezra Stiles went so far as to argue that George Washington was America's Joshua. "The United States elevated to Glory and Honor. A sermon preached before His Excellency Jonathan Trumbull, Esq. L.L.D. Governor and Commander in Chief, and the Honorable General Assembly of the State of Connecticut, Convened at Hartford, at the Anniversary Election, May 8, 1783," in *Pulpit of the American Revolution*, ed. J. W. Thornton (New York: Cap, reprint 1970 [1860]), 403, 439, 443.

3. Ludwig Feuerbach, *The Essence of Christianity*, trans. G. Eliot (Buffalo, N.Y.: Prometheus Books, 1989 [1841]).

4. The myth that America is a nation destined by God to bring freedom to the world is a secularized version of one of the foundation myths that have shaped the American mind—the myth of America as "a millennial nation." See Hughs, *Myths America Lives By*, especially chap.4.

5. As Jewett and Lawrence note, beginning in the 1960s, leaders (Kennedy and Johnson especially) began to add to the national civil religious confidence of a messianic calling to free people, "the belief in [America's] own superpower." Jewett and Lawrence, *Captain America and the Crusade against Evil*, 102. This motif, they argue, has taken on very dangerous apocalyptic connotations in recent times. Also instructive is Jewett and Lawrence's observation that devotion to the flag has taken on religious connotations, especially in the proposed constitutional amendment to prohibit "the physical desecration of the flag." (See ibid., chap. 15). Only something sacred can be *de*-secrated.

6. Israel has stumbled, Paul says, but it has not been rejected (Rom. 11:1–2, 11, 28–29). God is using their national disobedience as the occasion to reach the Gentiles and will use the faith of Gentiles to win back the Jewish nation (11:11–15, 25, 30–31). Paul is confident that in the end Israel as a nation will return to God and be saved (Rom. 11:26). For an insightful discussion of the role of Israel in Paul's thought, see James D. G. Dunn, *The Theology of Paul the Apostle* (Grand Rapids, Mich.: Eerdmans, 1998), 499–532.

7. In this sense Jesus—and therefore the church—is both the fulfillment and the replacement of Israel's nationalistic mission. On Jesus as the new Israel, see N. T. Wright, *The Climax of the Covenant: Christ and the Law in Pauline Theology* (Minneapolis: Fortress, 1992), esp. 18–40.

8. See, for example, Ray Comfort, *How to Win Souls and Influence People* (Gainesville, Fla.: Bridege-Logos, 1999); Ray Comfort, *Revival's Golden Key* (Gainesville, Fla.: Bridge-Logos, 2002); Kirk Cameron and Ray Comfort, *The Way of the Master* (Wheaton, Ill.: Tyndale, 2002).

9. This of course doesn't imply that confrontational evangelism *never* works. It sometimes does. But when it does, I suspect it's usually with people who happen to already share, if only subconsciously, the presuppositions of the evangelist (viz. breaking a commandment warrants eternal hell).

CHAPTER 9: CHRISTIANS AND VIOLENCE: CONFRONTING THE TOUGH QUESTIONS

1. See Wink, *The Powers That Be*, 99–100.

2. Ibid., 111.

3. For a critical overview of various interpretations, see Richard Hays, *The Moral Vision of the New Testament: Community, Cross, New Creation*

(San Francisco: HarperSanFrancisco, 1996), 319–29. Augustine's interpretation is particularly ingenious—or insidious. He contends that, "what is here required is not a bodily action, but an inward disposition." *Against Faustus*, 22.76, in O'Donovan and O'Donovan, *From Irenaeus to Grotius: A Sourcebook in Christian Political Thought, 100–1625* (Grand Rapids: Eerdmans, 1999), 118. In this way, Jesus' radical teachings get divorced from actual behavior, a concept that has plagued Christianity to this day. No one exposes the harm this impossible divorce has wrought in Christendom as well as Camp does in *Mere Discipleship*.

4. It should be noted that there are a number of issues we could raise at this point but that would take us outside the parameters of this book. For example, what of a Christian serving in a capacity where they might have to order a killing but not personally carry it out directly? What of Christians serving in a capacity where they make or supply the weapons that kill people? Indeed, what of Christians who pay taxes that fund the military that kills people? These are important questions, but I will have accomplished what I intended to accomplish with this book if I can simply help American kingdom-of-God people see the urgent need *to begin asking these questions*. The central problem with the American church today, I believe, is not that we haven't agreed on an answer to these ambiguous questions. Rather, it's that we are so steeped in nationalistic idolatry that we don't even think of seriously asking such questions in the first place!

5. For expositions, defenses, and critiques of the "just war" theory, see Paul Ramsey, *War and the Christian Conscience* (Durham, N.C.: Duke University, 1961); Paul Ramsey, *The Just War: Force and Political Responsibility* (New York: University Press of America, reprint, 1983); William F. Stevenson, *Christian Love and Just War: Moral Paradoxes and Political Life in St. Augustine and His Modern Interpreters* (Macon, Ga.: Mercer University, 1987); Robert G. Clouse, ed., *War: Four Christian Views* (Downers Grove, Ill.: InterVarsity, rev. ed. 1991); Lisa Sowle Cahill, *Love Your Enemies: Discipleship, Pacifism, and Just War Theory* (Minneapolis: Fortress, 1994); Richard J. Regan, *Just War: Principles and Cases* (Washington D.C.: Catholic University of America, 1996). For expositions and defenses of various pacificist positions, see J. H. Yoder, *Nevertheless: The Varieties of Religious Pacifism* (Scottdale, Penn.: Herald, 1971); J. H. Yoder, *The Original Revolution: Essays on Christian Pacifism* (Scottdale, Penn.: Harold, 1971);

S. Hauweras, *The Peaceable Kingdom: A Primer in Christian Ethics* (Notre Dame, Ind.: University of Notre Dame, 1983); S. Hauweras, *Against the Nations: War and the Survival in a Liberal Society* (Minneapolis: Winston Press, 1985); Jacques Ellul, *Violence: Reflections from a Christian Perspective* (New York: Seabury, 1969); Arthur Weinberg and Lila Weinberg, *Instead of Violence* (Boston, Mass.: Beacon Press, 1963); Dale W. Brown, *Biblical Pacifism: A Peace Church Perspective* (Elgin, Ill.: Brethren, 1986).

6. George Zabelka, "I Was Told It Was Necessary," [Interview] *Sojourners* (9/8, 1980), 14.

7. Yoder, *The Politics of Jesus*, 198. See also Hays, *Moral Vision*, 320–31.

8. For example, it is no longer disputable that the Nixon administration kept U.S. soldiers fighting in Vietnam well after the decision to evacuate was made for the purpose of preserving appearances until after the election. Thousands of U.S. soldiers as well as Vietnamese soldiers and civilians were killed during this interval. See Jewett and Lawrence, *Captain America*, 279–85. Similarly, many argue that the present war in Iraq was waged, intentionally or unintentionally, under false pretenses. We all now know that Iraq posed no "imminent threat" to the United States, as most within the United Nations insisted prior to the war.

9. For an insightful discussion on how easy it is to be deceived about the necessity or justifiability of violence, see in L. Tolstoy, *The Kingdom of God*, chap. 12.

10. Camp, *Mere Discipleship*, 148. For a discussion of various texts sometimes cited to argue that Jesus was not unequivocally against violence, see Hays, *Moral Vision*, 332–37.

11. The second-century pagan Celsus argued against Origen that if all people behaved as Christians (in the second century) behaved—loving their enemies, refusing to engage in violence, etc.—"the affairs of the earth would fall into the hands of the wildest and most lawless barbarians." Cited by Origen, "Against Celsus," 8.68 in *Ante-Nicene Fathers*, vol. 4., ed. A. Roberts and J. Donaldson (Peabody, Mass.: Hendrickson, reprint 1999 [1885]), 665. Origen rightly pointed out that if *everybody* acted as Jesus taught, there would be no "lawless barbarians." Ibid., 666. It should be noted that the dialogue demonstrates that second-century Christians were generally known for their refusal to engage in violence. It should also be noted that, once Christianity acquired the power of Caesar and became "Christendom," Church

theologians used Celsus's pagan line of reasoning to insist that Christians *can't* be expected to take the New Testament's teaching against violence seriously—at least to the point of denying there's a "just war" exception to it. See Camp, *Mere Discipleship*, 37–39.

12. See W. Wink, *Jesus and Nonviolence: A Third Way* (Minneapolis: Fortress, 2003), 1–2.

13. Tertullian, "Apology," *Ante-Nicene Fathers*, vol. 3, 55.

We want to hear from you. Please send your comments about this book to us in care of zreview@zondervan.com. Thank you.

GRAND RAPIDS, MICHIGAN 49530 USA

ZONDERVAN.COM/
AUTHORTRACKER